STREET JEWELLERY

New Cavendish Books

DEDICATED
TO MAVIS

Street Jewellery was first published in 1978
Revised and enlarged edition published in 1988
Companion edition – More Street Jewellery ISBN 0 904568 39 3 H/B
ISBN 0 904568 47 4 S/B

Designed by Badge Group Design, Newcastle upon Tyne
in association with John Cooper

Editorial Direction – Allen Levy and Narisa Chakra

Cover Enamel Sign, Garnier Signs, London
Colour separations, Aragorn, London
Setting and mono illustrations, Wyvern Typesetting Ltd, Bristol

New Cavendish Books
3 Denbigh Road, London W11 2SJ

Printed in Shekou, China

ISBN 0 904568 16 4   (S/B ISBN 0 904568 21 0)

Contents

Preface

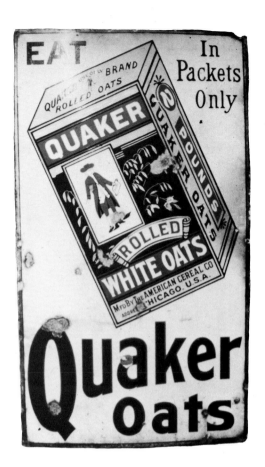

'Street Jewellery' has gained such popularity since it was published in 1978 (originally to catalogue our touring exhibition '100 Years of Enamel Signs', and remaining the authoritative work on enamelled iron advertising signs ever since), that we here offer an enlarged and revised edition of that work.

This comprises many newly discovered, previously unpublished items, combined with material from 'More Street Jewellery' (1982), and from various periodicals, plus extracts from foreign books on the subject, added to the essential original text of 'Street Jewellery'.

The response to 'Street Jewellery' proved that enamel advertising signs, which up to that time had been the preserve of a few dedicated dealers, collectors and photographers, had a wide, general appeal. This reached out to the general collectors of advertising ephemera (who could augment their specialisation, such as bottles, with a few well chosen signs), to the enthusiast for social history who could find fresh evidence of the social forms and functions of this kind of street advertising. But most of all the vast majority of the older general public, for whom the medium was a living memory, took to the book because of the pleasant nostalgic reveries they experienced by seeing these once-familiar images again.

Stimulation of interest in the subject has also been evinced by the number of products produced by commercial enterprises directly inspired by 'Street Jewellery', including reproduction signs, miniature signs for model railways, wallpaper and gift-wrapping paper, all based on our book illustrations, and sign collection. But perhaps the ultimate mark of the 'arrival' of the activity of collecting enamel advertising signs, as an independent phenomenon inspired by our two books, has been the inclusion of the term 'street jewellery' in the O.E.D Supplement (Vol. IV, '86) to denote the activity.

The fraternity of enamel sign collectors has grown into an international network of enamophiles, without whose cooperation and commitment we would not have been able to produce these books. We hope that this revised work, produced with their help, will encourage its readers to discover and preserve still further examples of fine street jewellery, and that even more exciting finds will come to light, to fuel the ever-growing enthusiasm for the subject.

The membership of the enamel sign collectors' club, The Street Jewellery Society, which we founded in 1983, encourages this aim, and welcomes new members.

C.B. & A.M.
Newcastle upon Tyne

Acknowledgements

A book of this kind can only be prepared with the assistance and cooperation of many individuals and organisations. It is not possible to give detailed or proportional credit to all the people who have helped us over the years, but it is with great gratitude that we acknowledge the generous and selfless assistance of the many collectors, photographers, dealers and manufacturers, plus of course numerous shop-keepers and members of the public who have contributed material help to us in our endeavours.

Listed here are the names of just some of the kind people to whom we owe a debt of gratitude.

We would like to pay fond tribute to Audrey Baglee and Geoffrey Morley, and to thank all other relatives and friends for their continued encouragement and support.

Ian Allen, Brian Anderson, John Anderson, Badge Group Design, R. Bamberough, R. Barker, A. G. Barr (Tizer), Bass Museum, Colin Baxter, Beamish North of England Open Air Museum, Ivor Beard, L'Emaillerie Belge, Jeremy Biggs, Peter Birch, Mick Blackburn, Alan Blakeman, Bluebell Railway, Blue Circle Group, Françoise Bourdillion-Grima, Bourton-on-the-Water Motor Museum, BBC Television, G. Braekman – Society for Environmental Cultural Care (Vereniging vor Kulterele Milieuzorg VZW, Gent), BP Oil, Brooke Bond Oxo, David Brown, David C. C. Brown, J. W. Brown, Bryant & May, Burmah–Castrol, Burnham Signs (Onyx), Roy Burton, Steve Burton, Bob Buxton, L.P.C., Causey Antiques, Mike Cavanagh, Nat Chait, Geoffrey Clarke, Collectors Mart Magazine, Colman's Foods, Birgitta Conradson, Joe & Sue Cussen, Christel Cuypers, Daily Express, Daily Mirror, Paul Davies, Mary Dixon, Dodo Old Advertising, Graham Douglas, John Dove, Eddie Dunks, Eddie Dunne, Graham Eastwood, Enamelled Iron Signs, Esso Petroleum, Tom Falconer, Liz Farrow, Derek & Vera Faulkner, Ulrich Feuerhorst, Finlay & Thompson, Mick & Jackie Forbes, Stan Foster, John Gall & Rosy Allan, Garnier Signs, Bob Gibson, Jim Gilroy, Geoffrey Goddard, Goodyear Tyre & Rubber, Christopher Gordon, Erica Gorman, Richard Green, David Griffith & Josephine Wright, David E. Griffiths, Alan Grimes, Mark Handy, Michael Harris, John Hawkins, Hawthorn Garage, Heinz, Paul Heyd, J. R. Hill, Alan Hooper, Hovis, Bill Humphrey, Ingersoll, Ironbridge Gorge Museum, Irvine Motors, Ed Jaques, Mick Jones, Ken King, Judi Kirk, Spyros Kypriotis, Philip John, Leo Lambert, Allen Levy, Lens of Sutton, Stafford Linsley, Leslie Longstaff, Maurice Lovett, Lyons, Geoff Marston, Mabel & Mr. Bennett, Hon. Bill McAlpine, N. Van Maldegen, K. A. Maskall, Mills & Allen, Mobil Oil, Janet Moody, Somerset Moore, Roy Morgan, Llyn E. Morris, Bob Mouland, Dave Nelson, Olle Nessle, Newcastle City Libraries, Newcastle Evening Chronicle, City of Newcastle upon Tyne, N.E. Cooperative Society, Mike Ockenden, Old Fashioned Cobbler, Robert Opie, Palethorpes, James Palm, Past Times, Pentalow, Philipson Studios, John & Sandie Phillips, John Piper, Barrie Pook, George Pope, Valerie Pragnall, Quaker Oats, Radio Times Hulton Picture Library, Howard & Valerie Raine, Reckitt & Colman, Relic Designs, Tom Richards, Stewart Rickards, Des Rolfe, Spencer Rutter, Sainsbury's, Scottish & Newcastle Breweries, Shell UK Oil, Adrian Shotton, Peter Simpkin, Smiler, Sir Frederick Sowrey, Spillers, Mike Standen, Star Cafe, Holge Steinle, Sterling Health, David Stevens, Jeff Stultiens, Neil Smith, Neville Summers, Susan J. Szczepanski, Steve & Elizabeth Taylor, Frank Thornton, Ian Trodd, Vaux Breweries, Maurice Turner, Tyne & Wear Industrial Monuments Trust, Tyne & Wear Museums Service, Tyne Tees Television, Simon Valedy, David Van der Plank, Vestry House Museum, Victoria & Albert Museum, Vitreous Enamel Development Council, Volkswagen GB, Meryl Wakeman, Keith Wakenshaw, Alan Wall, Simon Warden, Colin & Jacqui Ware, A. E. Warner, Donna Welsh, Martin White, Peter Williams, Walter Willson, C. D. Wilson, Michael Wlassikoff, Wolverhampton Central Library, Wolverhampton Polytechnic Department of Visual Communications, David Wood, Yorkshire Post.

Introduction

Street jewellery, flashing in the winter sunlight, gleaming in gaslight, washed by the rain, impervious to the grime of industrial towns, a hard fact reinforcing its message through total permanence – 'The Plate That Outlasts All Others'; ruby red and emerald green, sapphire blue, ivory white and ebony black, an abundance of reassuring text and opulent imagery every time you visited the corner shop – the enamel sign.

Until their recent functional decline and the redevelopment of their sites, enamelled iron signs were, from the 1880s until the 1950s, amongst the most striking features of drab industrial streets in most towns and villages around the country. Most people do not notice the signs that remain, since they are now neglected, and their messages are often irrelevant. But from railway stations to post offices, back street corner shops to warehouses, enamel signs are still to be found. Clean the dirt from the surface and they will be as bright as the day when they were put up, probably some fifty to one hundred years ago. The advertisers' names still stir the memories of our grandparents' generation: 'We used Van Houten's Cocoa when I was a lad', and the claims such as 'Craven "A" will not affect your throat' and 'Beecham's pills make all the difference' recall a time when the Trades Descriptions Act did not cramp the copywriter's style. We are surprised too by some of the prices such as 'Whitbread Ale and Stout – 2/6d a dozen' and 'Ingersoll watches from 5/-', which were peculiar to a pre-inflationary age; such quotations would not be made in such a permanent medium today. The Patent Enamel Company, formed in 1880, claimed their enamelled sheet iron as 'The plate that outlasts all others'. In an age of iron, it was iron that served every function. The enamel sign was the logical extension of the Victorian preoccupation with permanence and stability. A sheet of steel, coated in coloured glass, fixed by huge iron staples to a solid brick or stone wall, was the ideal public relations exercise. These signs implied that not only the manufacturer and his product, but also his advertised claims, would last forever. The

contemporary vogue for early advertising has brought in its wake a renewal of appreciation of the special qualities of the enamel sign.

This book attempts to present an outline of the historical, technical and visual elements of the enamel advertising medium.

Historical background and manufacturing techniques

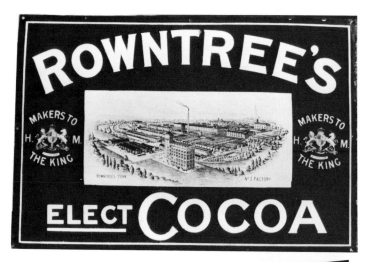

It was not until the early 1800s that porcelain enamelling on cast-iron was developed and practised in Central Europe. Later, around 1850, sheet iron manufacturing processes developed, porcelain enamelling was initiated in the United States and Britain.

In England, Benjamin Baugh, following a visit to Germany in 1857, started an enamelling business at premises in Bradford Street, Birmingham. Baugh took out a number of patents, from 1859 onwards, relating to the metal fabrication and enamelling process. He is described in the Patent Office register as 'Manager of Salt's Patent Enamel Works, Bradford Street, Birmingham'. It is understood that the first project undertaken by this company was making the decorated panels used on buildings and also on church altars. Decorated ceilings were supplied to the Gaekwar of Baroda, for the Durbar Hall in India, and also to the Kensington Museum* and a London railway terminal. This firm is also known to have had a stand at the 1860 Exhibition in London.

Salt's became a public company and, in 1889 built a large factory at Selly Oak, which was designed and laid out for the manufacture of enamelled iron signs under the name of the 'Patent Enamel Company Limited'. This was probably the first and only factory built specifically for sign-making. It had twelve furnaces for fusing the enamel, two scaling furnaces as the iron required to be scaled and stretched, and a large printing room, plus a huge area for steampipe drying. The company also smelted its own enamels and colour oxides. A railway siding ran into the factory, which also had its own canal arm and stables to accommodate horses.

A boom in enamelled signs came with the expansion of the railways, and orders for 100,000 signs were quite normal. Up to the time of World War I a vast quantity of signs was exported, but this market was lost as foreign countries, one by one, established their own enamelling firms.

* now accessible to view in the tea room of the V. & A.

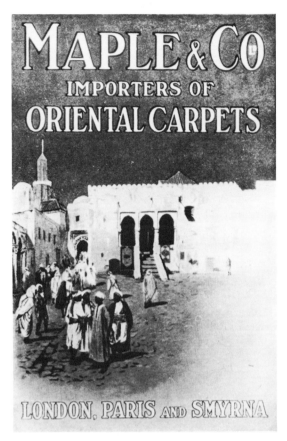

Following Baugh's lead, other firms sprang up throughout Britain. Some of the largest, whose names can still be found in the small print on many signs were Chromo of Wolverhampton, Imperial of Birmingham, The Falkirk Iron Co., and Bruton's, Burnham's, Garnier's and Wood & Penfold, all of London (p. 94).

It is recorded in Burnham's archives that when an advertiser commissioned a batch of signs, they usually specified that the sign-making company should be responsible for the distribution and fixing of the signs within a limited period from the time of manufacture. The railways facilitated distant distribution, which was then taken up by a local carrier with horse and cart who would deliver and install the signs.

The work of distributing Colman's signs fell to their Tableting Staff, whose job it was to negotiate sites, fix the plates and clean and maintain them at regular intervals. Rents, either in money or in goods were paid to the property owner for the privilege. The Tableting Staff operated from three depots strategically placed throughout the country and these duties entailed full-time employment. Today the number of signs left *in situ* is very small. An article in *The Junior Traveller. Journey the Tenth*, printed and published by the Hovis Bread Flour Co. in the summer of 1902, deals with the different forms of Hovis advertising and promotion and reads: '"Hovis food for babies and invalids" is a very nice plate 8 feet in length, with good clear letters that we supply for spaces under shop windows or any other bold position. We also have a similar plate for Hovis bread.'

Some of the earliest products to be advertised through the medium were animal foods – Thorley's, confectionery – Cadbury's, Fry's and Rowntree's, soaps – Hudson's, Pear's and tea – Mazawattee, Nectar and United Kingdom. Many high class stores and products were early users, e.g. Maples, Aquascutum and makers of pianos, but these prestigious signs seemed to disappear when the method became more widespread and vulgarised.

The hey-day of enamelled iron signs was comparatively short. They reached their peak before the 1914 War, went into decline from 1918, and their end was in sight by 1939. In the half century leading to World War II, millions of signs were produced. During the 1950s, however after a virtual halt of production in the previous decade, and with continued rationing of steel, there emerged a new and powerful rival in the form of huge hoardings, which not only masked the bomb sites, but also displayed the novel American-style photographic posters. World War II had struck the *coup de grace* to a dying industry by simultaneously destroying their main sites and thereby creating new show places for the rival medium. Furthermore, World War II and its aftermath, denied the sign manufacturers vital raw materials.

The porcelain enamel process involves the re-fusing of powdered glass on a metal surface via two principal processes.

Cast-iron, dry process enamels, were the first to be used on a large scale. In this process the castings were sand blasted to give them a clean surface. The grip or ground coat was then applied, and this comprised a powdered glass, clay and water suspension, with a consistency similar to that of cream. This was dipped, slushed and sprayed onto the cool casting and allowed to dry. The ware was then introduced into a furnace at about 900°C, and allowed to reach the temperature of the furnace. The hot ware was then withdrawn, and

powdered glass dusted through a screen onto it. This powdered glass melted as it fell on to the surface of the ware and formed a continuous layer, known as 'enamel'. Several applications were made in this way, the ware being returned to the furnace for reheating before each application.

The enamelling of iron only became possible because of the ability to vitreous-enamel sheet wrought iron, and it was not until the 1920s, when Armco produced a steel sufficiently free from defects, that sheet steel could be used for signs. Since that time, all orders for steel to be vitreous-enamelled, have been for specially produced 'vitreous-enamelling quality steel'. Sheet iron was

The Svea enamelworks, Sweden

Interior of Burnham's factory, showing kiln.

ordered as 'pure scotch wrought puddled iron', and sign makers were very sad when the last 'hearth' of this was produced by the Pather Iron & Steel Co. Limited. There was less wastage with iron, since all defects could be rectified during processing and the colours on iron were crystal clear, whereas those on steel – when closely compared – seemed to have a greasy appearance. Incidentally, collectors can easily differentiate between iron and steel signs as those made from iron have backs of a mid-grey colour and will invariably have swill lines; the backs of steel signs are blue-black and normally by the time steel was used in production, the base colour was sprayed and not swilled. In the factory the 'grip' coat was never named as such; it was always referred to as 'grey' and not changed to blue-black.

Sheet steel enamelling has become the process most widely used for porcelain enamels nowadays. In this way the sheet is put through a cleaning and pickling process which prepares the surface and also receives a ground coat, containing a small percentage of cobalt to give adhesion. This ground coat is applied by the wet process, is dried and then fired in a furnace at about 830°C. After the ware has been removed from the furnace and cooled a second coat of cover enamel is applied. This cover coat may be of any desired colour and may have special requirements or properties, depending on what use the ware is to be put. It is commonly dipped or sprayed onto the ware and then fired at a slightly lower temperature. Enamel colours are achieved by adding metallic oxides to the ground 'frit' or glasses at some stage, in greater or lesser percentages, according to the strength of the colour desired. Essentially some will be 'softer' than others and will burn out at high – or additional – firing temperatures. Consequently, the ground coat will be hardened by being applied first and receiving the most firings, while the softest colour is applied last, to receive the minimum number of firings at the lowest temperature. Thus firing temperatures will vary from something over 860°C to as low as 800°C for one sign.

Finally, the decoration is applied and fired into the last coat. This is done with a rubber stamp coated with ceramic colours in the form of inks or by dusting on a coloured pigment to an area stamped with gum or

varnish. There is also a process of transfer which uses a ceramic decal which enables the image to be attached to and fired into the ware. These transfers are often needed where a small piece of fine, intricate work, such as a coat of arms, trademark or instructions, is essential on an otherwise wholly lettered sign. This technique was a comparative late comer and as lithographic processes could achieve similar results, was little used.

Originally the design was applied by the use of stencils, but today this is principally applied for one-off orders where the cost of making screens outweighs the more labour-intensive stencil process. In this stencil process the colour was sprayed onto the plate and after drying, had the consistency of weak distemper. The stencils, cut to the appropriate design, were placed on the plate and the exposed colour brushed away, leaving the design intact. The plate was then fired and the colour vitrified indelibly into the background. This process could be carried out with successive colours, using further stencils, until the most intricate designs and patterns were achieved. It was a process which demanded a great deal of skill, not only on the part of the stencil cutters, but also from those 'brushing out' as they had to work accurately and carefully ensuring that they only brushed away the material that was unwanted without disturbing the surface of the colour that was intended to remain.

A design too complicated for the stencilling process was etched on to a stone for each colour and the stone was then placed in a printing press. A print on paper was then taken and the sheet – still wet with ink – was laid over the sign and peeled off leaving the wet printing ink on the surface. Dry enamel pigment was then dusted over the ink, leaving the design in colour to be fired.

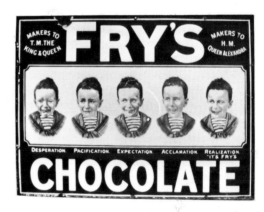

This process was repeated for all the colours. In the twenties, instead of paper, gelatine sheets were used which could be cleaned each time and zinc plates were introduced to replace the stone.

At the turn of the century a method of reproducing photographs in black or sepia on to vitreous enamel was invented. The monochrome Fry's Five Boys chocolate sign is an example of this process, while the coloured version is the same plate but tinted.

Today, however, much design application is carried out by the screen printing process. For this the enamel colour is specially formulated and ground into the form of ink which is then screened on to the steel plate. After screening the plate is fired. With this process it is possible to produce detail of great intricacy as well as multicoloured and pictorial designs, which would be impossible with the stencil method.

Locations
and Social
environment

'The Daily Mirror – Best All Along The Line', reminds us of the wide range of locations in which these signs appeared. In this case, beside a railway track or on a station, it was a response to the expansion of the railways which contributed a great deal to the development of the sign making industry. The railways made possible the shipment of huge orders and provided ready made locations and a captive public. 'W.H. Lever was a great believer . . . he even went to the trouble of choosing the exact sites where the enamel signs were to be displayed at railway stations; and the advantage of the right-hand against the left-hand of the booking office was carefully considered' (noted by Robert Opie in *The Ephemerist*, Vol. 1, No. 10, May 1977, from Professor Wilson's *History of Unilever*). Virol saw the value of station approaches in the early days and acquired most of these, lining the entrance or exit routes with their standard blue, white and orange signs and adding such authoritative slogans as 'nursing mothers need it' and although it would be hard to find any other form of advertising used by Virol, everyone was aware of the product. This company jealously guarded their sites, even after World War II, until it was no longer viable for them to renew their leases. It was the change to higher rents for advertising sites on railway stations that lost these locations to the enamel sign and made them far more suitable for paper posters. The first company to recognise the value of stair risers as locations for signs was Mazawattee Tea, followed by Ovum and Redferns and they were imitated in turn, especially on trams and omnibuses, by Iron Jelloids.

Trams and omnibuses were the other main forms of transport favoured by advertisers as sign sites, but some commercial vehicles were also used, being clad liberally with custom-made signs. On the trams and buses the signs were fixed to the stair balustrading, the stair risers, the backs of seats and the outer bodywork panels. On the streets along which these vehicles travelled were located the major static placements. The motoring garages (usually converted smithies or stables) which valued the signs as evidence of their modernity, and most important – shop fronts. These were mainly corner shops, general dealers, post offices, ironmongers, pubs, off-licences and the gable ends, walls or fences of other prominent buildings, located in the natural commercial centres of cities, towns and villages. In the countryside signs for the specialist agricultural products such as Thorley's pig food, Toogood's seeds, and Ransome's farming equipment might be seen on barns and farmhouses, and often they still survive because of their isolation.

Today, the constantly changing images confronting us on the street billboards make the enamel sign an anachronism. It goes against the grain for an advertiser to retain the same campaign on a long term basis; to do so would indicate a lack of enterprise or a non-expanding market.

This advertising practice of bombarding public awareness with constantly changing imagery, exploded

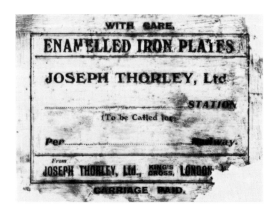

A large number of signs being erected at a garage in Theale, Berkshire c.1920. (From 'The Country Garage' by Llyn E. Morris)

with a vengeance in Britain after World War II. At this time most major cigarette manufacturers deliberately removed their old advertising signs from the walls, as did Reckitt's with their Nugget Boot Polish signs – and many were replaced with a new dynamic phase of 'contemporary' Festival-of-Britain graphics. These were sometimes still on enamel, e.g. Turf cigarettes, but more usually they were on disposable and replaceable paper or tin. These were, of course, not unique to the 50s, having never declined in popularity as an advertising medium since the invention of printing, but with the development of silkscreen and photolithographic techniques, the paper poster came into its own again to fulfil demands more economically than enamel with its obdurate permanency in an age where obsolescence was structured into the manufacture and advertisement of so many products.

The Town and Country Planning Act of 1947 added a further restraint in that all signs fitted above fascia level required the complicated process of obtaining planning permission before they could be displayed. This was hardly profitable and so the alternative was for enamels to be relocated as trestle or forecourt signs.

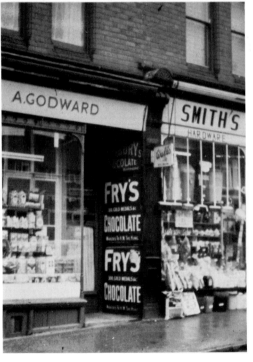

'The Tree of Knowledge' – photographed by John Piper in 1937

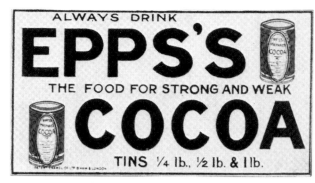

As evidence of changing social habits and conditions, the slogans and advertising claims on enamel signs are very instructive. A selection is given of some of the more exalted and outrageous of these, that could only have been made before the current age of advertising watchdogs.

'Craven ''A'' will not affect your throat'
'Beecham's Pills make all the difference'
'Van Houten's Cocoa, best and goes farthest'*
'Epps's Cocoa for strong and weak'
'Fry's Cocoa – there is no better food'
Pear's soap – 'Matchless for the complexion'
Oxo – 'Splendid with milk for children', 'Excellent with milk for growing children', 'Meat and drink to you', 'The perfect beef beverage'
Virol – 'Delicate children need it'

New Hudson cycles would climb any hill, but if you were not up to that kind of exertion you probably needed Wincarnis, which 'Gives New Life To The Invalid, New Strength To the Weak, Increased Vigour To Brain Workers, A Wealth of Health to Everyone. The World's Greatest Restorative In Cases of Anaemia: Depression: Brain Fag: Sleeplessness: Physical & Mental Prostration: Nerve Troubles: And in Convalescence.'

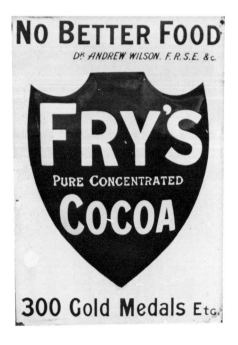

*James Blades, on page 53 of his autobiography, mentions a special use for this sign!

The next selection encouraged purchase by topical social comment, or appeal to class values:

'Bryan and May matches Support Home Industries, Employ British Labour'
'Simpson's whisky – as supplied to the House of Lords'
Hudson's soap 'For the People', 'Used in all "The Happy Homes Of England"'.
'Rinso, soak the clothes – that's all; saves coal every wash day'
'Nectar, the most economical tea sold'
'Lyon's tea, a packet for every pocket'
'Brooke Bond tea, spend wisely, save wisely'
'Lucas Batteries on extended credit terms.'

Thus the enamel sign reflected or created consumer demand both in colour and texture and unlike film or paper, remains an almost unblemished relic of its time.

The first area worth noting is where certain product types, frequently used and advertised at the turn of the century, have either been superseded by modern labour saving products, or do not warrant present day advertising. Before the current wave of medical discovery and State care, there was a great demand for health-giving tonics such as Wincarnis and Anti-Laria (non-alcoholic sparkling wine, 'a stimulant second only to champagne, at a fraction of the cost'), ginger wine, Beecham's pills and Liver Salts of various kinds. Before the advent of electric washing machines and biological

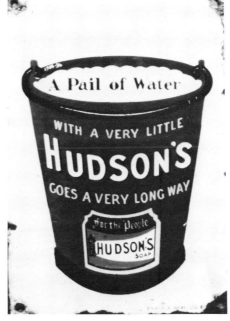

washing powders there were signs advertising 'mangling done here' and many brands of soap ranging from Sunlight and Hudson's Dry Soap, to Mrs. Volvolutum's 'no rubbing, no soaking!'. The extensive use of other common household products recorded in enamel, but now reduced in importance are Colman's and Robin starch, Reckitt's blue, Chiver's carpet soap, several makes of metal polish, liquid Brasso, Komo metal paste and grate polishes such as Zebo, Zebra and James Dome Black lead. It was common to find advertisements for newly invented articles which are now very rarely advertised, such as Ediswan lamp bulbs or of obsolescent products such as Royal Daylight and Pratt's lamp oils and Veritas gas mantles, as well as several manufacturers of gas and oil engines for generating electricity and for farming purposes.

The emphasis on advertising various beverages has now changed completely. We no longer find cocoa greatly promoted, let alone as a valuable source of food. However, in the late nineteenth and early twentieth centuries, several rival companies, Cadbury's, Epps's, Fry's, Lyon's, Rowntree's and Van Houten's all brought their cocoa prominently to the notice of the public. Nor

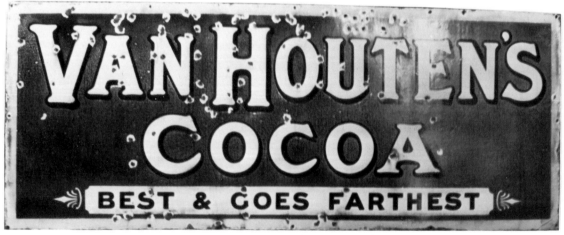

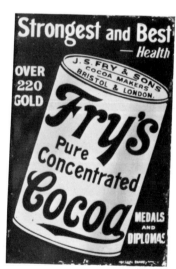

is tea so widely publicised today, except by a few major companies, yet during the period mentioned previously, Blue Cross, Brooke Bond, Horniman's, Lipton's, Lyon's, Mazawattee, Melrose's, Nectar, Silverbrook, Typhoo, United Kingdom and many more were all in serious rivalry through the medium of the enamel sign. At the same time only one instant coffee company was blowing its trumpet – 'Don't be misled, Camp Coffee is the best.' – Competitors remained silent, hardly the case today!

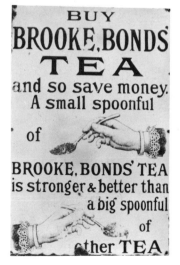

Blaydon Station 1911

Design, Texture, Typestyles and Stencil Patterns

The design concept for enamel advertising signs, having originated in the mid-Victorian era, largely retained the visual qualities of the early days throughout a century of major production. More than a score of sign manufacturers, some with their own designers, put out hundreds, even thousands, of individual designs, reproduced each time in hundreds or thousands in the permanent medium of glass fused to steel. Although most of the artists responsible for the creation of these designs have remained anonymous, their styles can sometimes be recognised in different signs, and attribution can be reinforced by the occasional inclusion of the manufacturer's name on the bottom corner of a sign, leading one to the recognition of a 'house style'. The products of Chromo of Wolverhampton, and Patent Enamel of Birmingham are especially easy to identify.

The many companies involved – most now defunct – included not only those mentioned above, but also The Imperial Enamel Company of Birmingham, The Falkirk Iron Company and Jordan's of Bilston; all these companies' work exhibiting high design standards. Few documents record the output of enamel sign manufacturers, but some surviving catalogues demonstrate the pride that each firm took in showing off its quality of design. Interesting adjuncts to these catalogues are two trade sample signs produced by Chromo and Patent at the turn of the century (illustrated in colour). These samples are quite charming as artefacts in themselves, and while not being 'genuine' advertisements, nevertheless illustrate the qualities and potential of the product being advertised, namely the signs themselves, by clearly demonstrating the available colours and techniques. Actually the colours used in these particular signs are not really representative of those generally chosen by advertisers. More often the primary shades of blue, red and yellow, reinforced by stark black and white, were employed. Less frequently used were the luxury colours brown, green, orange, maroon and cerulean blue; only the most expensive and elaborate signs made use of the exotic pastel and pale earth colours incorporated in the Chromo and Patent samples.

Although most of the designers have, as stated, remained anonymous – probably because of their low status as employees of an advertiser or sign manufacturer, a few celebrated names have remained linked to certain signs. The popularity of the new wave of English designers at the turn of the century in book illustration, newspaper advertising, theatre and travel posters, etc., made them attractive as designers to the enamel advertising sign trade.

Aubrey Beardsley was the progenitor of this new style, but alas, as far as we know, there are no enamels by his hand extant. However enamels survive from

several of his followers and imitators, including some by the Beggarstaffs (the pseudonym of Sir William Nicholson and James Pryde), John Hassall, Tom Browne, Septimus E. Scott and (better known as a horse painter than a designer) Sir Alfred Munnings. The essence of their style, now known as 'poster style' normally consists of opposing tones captured in a sinuous line. The flavour is reminiscent of the crude chap book woodcut blended with the more refined Japanese woodcut, and laced together by Art Nouveau. A combination of the visual results of these relief print techniques (as distinct from their means of production), when applied to the design of an enamel sign, was particularly appropriate, as the stencilling method of producing an enamel sign is essentially very similar in its visual qualities. Examples of pure black and white tonality are the c.1905 P. & R. Hay crinolined ladies by J. W. Simpson, the 'Three Generations' design for Rowntree's Elect Cocoa of 1899 (originally a poster by the Beggarstaffs) and the anonymous continental RVS insurance sign. Of similar technique and style, but incorporating areas of plain colour in black lines, are Hassall's Morse's Distemper series and Bibby's Cream Equivalent usually attributed to Tom Browne. Tom Browne certainly produced interesting lithographic images for Fry's chocolate which, having a full tonal range (originally designed for paper posters) and still redolent of the late Victorian, early Edwardian taste, for picturesque simplification. The power of this 'So near . . .' sign as a black and white image is highlighted when it is contrasted with the aesthetically unsuccessful attempt to produce a colour washed version. Far more successful as a colour design is the delightfully bold and humorous concept of a publican devised for Bullards Beers by Munnings. A late example of the flat bold colour and black line style is the famous W. H. Smith 'Newsboy' designed by Septimus E. Scott in the late 1920s.

Designers would obviously have enjoyed exploiting new enamelling effects as these became available; a few examples of innovative techniques in use follow:

Direct photographic transfers, sometimes combined with hand tinting, were used, in for example the beautiful Player's Navy Cut 'Actress', and without tinting, but with subtle retouching, the Jones' Sewing Machine 'Busy . . .' seamstress. Early examples of airbrushing are detectable on the British Dominions sports car sign, and on the Player's Navy Cut 'Hero's' lifebelt. We have also discovered, on a particularly well-preserved coloured Fry's 'Five Boys', the use of direct brush applied enamel colour, to enhance lithographed print, and brushwork additions can also be observed on the stencilled images of the 6'×4' Palethorpes and British Dominions signs.

31

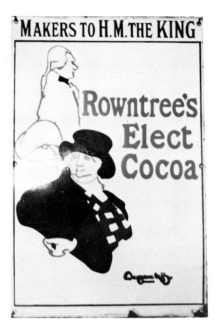

REMOVALS AND STORING.
HUDSONS
VICTORIA STATION, LONDON, S.W.
BRIGHTON, EASTBOURNE, PARIS.
ESTIMATES FREE

WE CLOSE AT
TO-DAY
HUDSONS
SOAP

COCHRAN&Co
BLUE BLACK
WHITING INK
COCHRAN & Co
LIVERPOOL & LONDON
BRITISH MANUFACTURE
Cochran's
Inks.

RUDGE-WHITWORTH
CYCLES
£5.5.0 to £15.15.0
RUDGE-WHITWORTH LTD
COVENTRY
BRITAIN'S BEST BICYCLE

BUTLER'S
ALES & STOUT
BIRMINGHAM

AGENT FOR
ROBBIALAC
PAINTS

Bovril
Makes
Contented
Cooks

MONSTERS
1 D
PINT

THE
"RAJAH"
CIGAR
2 D
EACH
7 /
FOR 1/
SEE THAT EACH CIGAR BEARS THE
NAME ON THE REGISTERED STAR BAND

BOAR'S
HEAD
TOBACCO

Smoke NUT
BROWN
For that
Nutty Flavour

Stephens'
Gum
STICKS QUICKLY

PURE FOOD
ESTD 57 1869
HEINZ
VARIETIES
PRODUCTS

PICKFORDS
REMOVALS & STORAGE
ENQUIRE WITHIN

GOLDEN
SHRED
MARMALADE
ROBERTSON. ONLY MAKER

WRIGHT'S
COAL TAR
SOAP
"For Skins
Like Mine"

MORRIS'S
BLUE
BOOK
MIXED
CIGARETTES
3 D PER PACKET OF 10
Every Packet Contains
Two Turkish,
Two Virginia,
One Russian,
One Havana,
Two Egyptian,
One Amber-Tipped Virginia,
One Gold-Tipped Virginia.

CADBURY'S
COCOA ESSENCE
REGISTERED
GUARANTEED PURE COCOA

DEPÔT FOR
"SWAN"
FOUNTPENS

DRINK
TAYLORS'
"PERFECTION
BRAND
8
GOLD MEDALS
HOP
BITTERS & STOUT
· IT IS THE BEST ·

Hudson's
Soap
ADVERTISING WAR
BALLOON
HUDSON'S
SOAP

SOW YOUR LAWN
Carters
TESTED SEEDS

MACDONALD'S
GLASGOW.
"KILTY" BRAND
Cut Golden Bar
In 1, 2 & 4 oz. Decorated Tins.

STEPNEY
TWO BRITISH GRIPPERS
TYRES

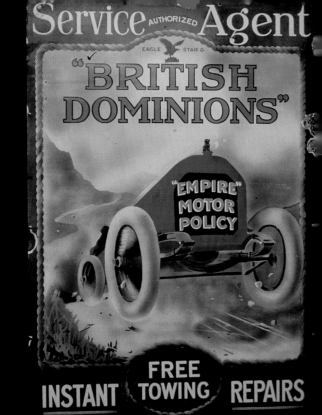

Service AUTHORIZED Agent
"BRITISH DOMINIONS"
"EMPIRE" MOTOR POLICY
FREE TOWING
INSTANT REPAIRS
ASSETS EXCEED
£19,000,000.

HUSH!! HE'S BUSY
PASSING SHOW

St. JULIEN
TOBACCO & CIGARETTES

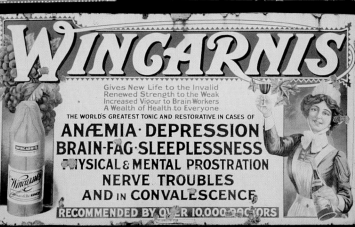

WINCARNIS
Gives New Life to the Invalid
Renewed Strength to the Weak
Increased Vigour to Brain Workers
A Wealth of Health to Everyone
THE WORLD'S GREATEST TONIC AND RESTORATIVE IN CASES OF
ANÆMIA · DEPRESSION
BRAIN · FAG · SLEEPLESSNESS
PHYSICAL & MENTAL PROSTRATION
NERVE TROUBLES
AND IN CONVALESCENCE
RECOMMENDED BY OVER 10,000 DOCTORS

THE PATENT ENAMEL CLD
SELLY OAK · BIRMINGHAM
SAMPLES OF COLOURS

LITTLE'S SHEEP DIPS
When you buy Little's Dips you are Buying
certain results — after using them you have
given your Stock absolute protection against
diseases that are certain to prove a source
of financial loss if allowed to gain a "foot-
hold" at all. Yet the cost of this protection
with Little's Dips is insignificant, and the
protection so complete that they are
APPROVED BY THE WORLD'S LEADING FLOCKMASTERS.
MORRIS, LITTLE & SON, LTD.
DONCASTER.

Buy Punch
— For all the best jokes

EDWARDS' DESICCATED SOUP
REGISTERED
Tomato
TOMATO.

Lyons' Cocoa

SPRINKLER TOPS
2D
6D
& LARGER TINS
ALADDIN
LIQUID METAL POLISH
SHINES BRIGHTEST AND LONGEST
PRIZE COUPON ATTACHED TO EACH TIN.

PLAYER'S
PLAYER'S NAVY CUT CIGARETTES
NAVY CUT CIGARETTES

RAILWAY ADVERTISING
MATCHLESS PUBLICITY
LONDON W.C.2
ADVERTISEMENTS
SEEN BY MILLIONS
DAILY.
W·H·SMITH & SON
CAN SUPPLY & EXHIBIT AN ADVERTISEMENT
THE SIZE OF THIS PLATE (50 × 30)
at the rate of 1/6 per week
Apply for Particulars to
18 JAMES ST. LIVERPOOL.

SUTER HARTMANN & RAHTJENS COMPOSITION Co Ltd
18 BILLITER STREET · LONDON ·

ANTIFOULING TRADE MARK COMPOSITIONS
PAINTS FOR ALL PURPOSES

EAT
PALETHORPES
PORK PIES

FRESH
TO-DAY

NUGGET
BOOT POLISH

WATERPROOFS
AND
PRESERVES
THE LEATHER

"CAMWAL"
LIKE THE BRITISH FLEET
"FIRST IN ALL WATERS"

SCIENCE
FLOOR
POLISH

HALIFAX
THE WORLD'S LARGEST
BUILDING SOCIETY

STRENGTH
SECURITY
SERVICE

HEAD OFFICE,
PERMANENT BUILDINGS, HALIFAX.

LONDON OFFICE.
HALIFAX HOUSE, 51–55, STRAND, W.C.2.

LIVE UNDER
YOUR OWN
ROOF

C.W.S. SOAP
CONGRESS
FOR ALL PURPOSES.

Wellington Journal & Shrewsbury News.
Read by a quarter of a Million.

500 Situations Vacant and Wanted.
Advertised every Saturday.

*"I did
and I'm contented!"*

PAGE & OVERTON'S
BREWERY LIMITED

2/6
PER DOZ

Trade
Mark

OATMEAL STOUT
SHIRLEY BREWERY CROYDON

EXTREME PRESSURE OIL ACTIVATOR AND CARBON REPELLENT

TUNE
UP
YOUR
ENGINE

RED X EX

TOP
UP
YOUR
SUMP

ADD TO OIL AND PETROL

PICKERINGS *Limited*
MAKERS
GLOBE ELEVATOR WORKS
STOCKTON-ON-TEES

OGDEN'S
"GUINEA
GOLD"
CIGARETTES

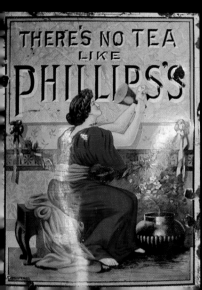

THERE'S NO TEA
LIKE
PHILLIPS'S

A Pail of Water

WITH A VERY LITTLE
HUDSON'S
GOES A VERY LONG WAY

HUDSON'S

**JOHNNIE
WALKER**
WHISKY

Born
1820 —

Still
going
Strong

NOW OLDER & BETTER THAN EVER

PUBLIC BAKERY
SETS IN
TO-DAY

For the People

HUDSON'S
SOAP

OGDENS
GUINEA
GOLD
CIGARETTES

Smith's
PINEWOOD
Cigarettes

"And they'd hardly
any Milk"

BIBBY'S CREAM
EQUIVALENT did it

3d
Per Packet

SUPPORT
HOME
TRADE

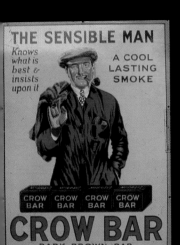

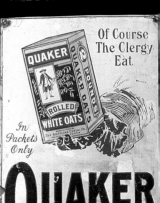

A PROPOSAL for Every Lady TO MAKE Delicious Custards WITH BIRD'S CUSTARD POWDER

THE BLACKSTONE OIL ENGINES

BLACKSTONE & Co L?. STAMFORD. ENGLAND.

For your throats sake smoke

Ask for HUDSON'S DRY SOAP

HUDSON'S ESTABLISHED OVER 50 YEARS

QUAKER

PURE

OATS

O'MARA'S Bacon & Hams

LIMERICK

WEBBS' SEEDS FOR ALL CLIMATES

Waterman's Ideal Fountain Pen.

BRASSO

BRASSO

METAL Polish

HOLDFAST BOOTS.

Bear Brand Swiss Milk

SMOKE SMITH'S GLASGOW

SOLD IN THREE STRENGTHS

MIXTURE

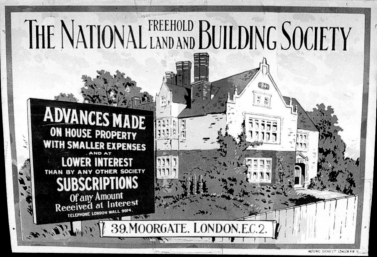

THE NATIONAL FREEHOLD LAND AND BUILDING SOCIETY

ADVANCES MADE ON HOUSE PROPERTY WITH SMALLER EXPENSES AND AT LOWER INTEREST THAN BY ANY OTHER SOCIETY SUBSCRIPTIONS Of any Amount Received at Interest
TELEPHONE LONDON WALL 9974.

39. MOORGATE. LONDON. E.C.2.

HUDSON'S Extract of SOAP

THE "GREYS"
10 CIGARETTES
SILK CUT VIRGINIA CIGARETTES
MANUFACTURED BY MAJOR DRAPKIN & COMPANY
20 for 1/-
"GREYS" ARE GREAT!

GOOD BROTHERS MARMION WORKS

THE "MARMION" Self Setter.
IS A TRUE ECONOMIZER
RAPID AND RELIABLE,
WILL HEAT A BATH
BEST IN VALUE,
LOWEST IN PRICE.
GENERAL CATALOGUE, MAILED FREE ON RECEIPT OF TRADE CARD

MANUFACTURERS. MERCHANTS AND SHIPPERS OF ALL BUILDING REQUISITES.

WALTHAMSTOW LONDON

DAIRY.-GUILDFORD

THE WEST SURREY CENTRAL DAIRY C°S
PURE RICH THICK
CREAM
93 Highest Honours.
28 Gold Silver & Bronze Medals
CHICAGO

PURITAN SOAP

"Pure as the Breeze"

PARAPLUIE-REVEL

Brauhaus Zinkelsbühl

Echtes Rumbacher

HUSQVARNA
MOTORCYKLAR

Persil
Persil

ROOKT
vROSSEM'S
TROOST

ENGRAIS D'AUBY

EN VENTE ICI

WECK

DAS BÜRGSCHAFTS-ZEICHEN
FÜR UNERREICHTE GÜTE
ANERKANNTE VERKAUFSTELLE

CHOCOLAT

DELESPAUL-HAVEZ
EN VENTE ICI

WIKLUNDS

AROME Maggi POTAGES
pour corser à la minute
MAGGI
Tubes de
CONSOMMÉ DÉJEUNER
au cacao-gluten

Denkt
AAN
NEGRI
CAUS-SEUR PRODUCT

Für alle Wäsche
Persil

Wohl-
bekomms

KRONENBRÄU
OFFENBURG

Schmidt'sche Wolle

BERGENBIER

Persil

Böninger
Rhein-Perle

ΖΥΘΟΣ
ΦΙΞ

CHOCOLAT
MENIER

ÉVITER LES
CONTREFAÇONS

MAGGI's
PRODUKTER

Gangloff

över
hela Sverige
GEVALIA kaffe

AMBRE
SOLAIRE

LE
BOUILLON
KUB
EXIGER
LE K
10¢
EN VENTE
ICI

Perlesreuter
Schmalzler
SORTEN: 0,00 und FRESK

WETTIG GEDEPONEERD

WOLLEN AaBe DEKENS
100% WOL
VOORKOMEN RHEUMATIEK
TILBURG HOLLAND

ΟΔΟΝΤΟΠΑΣΤΑ
ΧΛΩΡΟΔΟΝΤ

EXIGEZ
LE
BOUILLON
OXO
DE LA COMPⁱᵉ
LIEBIG
10⁵
BOUILLON
OXO

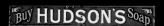

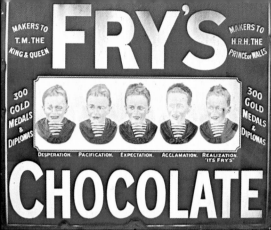

Wincarnis

THE WORLD'S GREATEST WINE TONIC AND NERVE RESTORATIVE

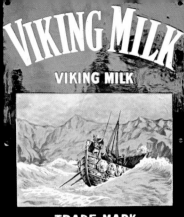

VIKING MILK

VIKING MILK

TRADE MARK

LATTE VIKING

PLAYER'S

Navy Cut Cigarettes

NATIONAL · BENZOLE · MIXTURE

WHEEL · BRAND

Gossages Dry Soap

SUN INSURANCE OFFICE

AD. 1710.

DRIVE WITH THE Sun BEHIND YOU

In Fine Powder

HUDSON'S DRY SOAP

Used in all the "Happy Homes of England"

HUDSON'S

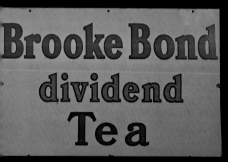

Brooke Bond dividend Tea

WE SELL SEALED Shell

WE SELL

Lyons

2d FRUIT PIES

MANY VARIETIES

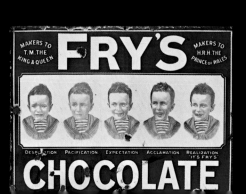

MAKERS TO T.M.THE KING & QUEEN

FRY'S

MAKERS TO H.R.H. THE PRINCE of WALES

DESPERATION   PACIFICATION   EXPECTATION   ACCLAMATION   REALIZATION IT'S FRY'S

CHOCOLATE

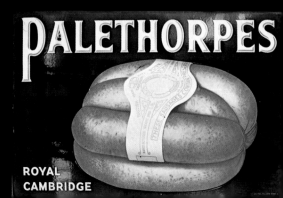

PALETHORPES

ROYAL CAMBRIDGE

JOHN SINCLAIR'S
RUBICON
TWIST

Player's Please

PLAYER'S NAVY CUT CIGARETTES MEDIUM
"It's the Tobacco that Counts"

WESTWARD HO!
SMOKING MIXTURE
"WESTWARD HO" SMOKING MIXTURE W.D. & H.O. WILLS
W.D. & H.O. WILLS

ROWNTREE'S ELECT COCOA
MAKERS TO T.M. THE KING & QUEEN.

SPRATT'S
SPRATT'S 'builds up' a dog!
DOG CAKES : BONIO : MIXED OVALS : WEETMEET

BLUE BAND MARGARINE

BRASSO
METAL Polish.

MAKERS TO H.M. THE KING.
ROWNTREE'S
CHOCOLATES
AND
PASTILLES
MAKERS TO H.M. THE QUEEN.

WILLS'S
STAR
STAR
Cigarettes
W.D. & H.O. WILLS
Bristol & London
CIGARETTES

WILLS'S
WOODBINES

AGENT FOR
THOMSON'S
DYE
WORKS
PERTH

VERITAS MANTLES
FOR
STRENGTH & BRILLIANCE.

DAGENITE
THE DEPENDABLE
ACCUMULATORS
SOLD HERE

FRESH
PALETHORPES
TO-DAY

Stephens
Inks
FAHRENHEIT CENTIGRADE
140 60
130
120 50
110 40
BLOOD 100 HEAT
90 30
80
70 20
HEALTH 60 TEMPER-
50 ATURE
40 10
FREEZ. 30 0 ING
20 10
10
0
FOR ALL
TEMPERATURES
Stephens
Inks

CHURCHMAN'S
"TORTOISESHELL"
TORTOISESHELL
SMOKING MIXTURE
SMOKING MIXTURE.

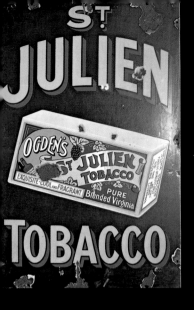

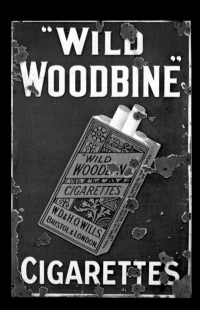

OXO
IT'S 'MEAT & DRINK' TO YOU
OXO CUBE · OXO CUBE

MELOX
DOG FOODS

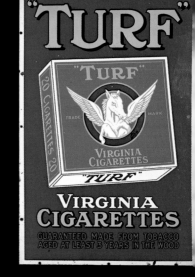
"TURF"
20 CIGARETTES 20
VIRGINIA CIGARETTES
TRADE MARK
"TURF"
VIRGINIA CIGARETTES
GUARANTEED MADE FROM TOBACCO
AGED AT LEAST 3 YEARS IN THE WOOD

Britax
SAFETY BELT FITTING SERVICE

BATTLEAXE BAR

OGDEN'S **WALNUT PLUG**
SWEET AS A NUT

BOVRIL
Oh Mamma
don't forget to order BOVRIL

Smoke
PLAYER'S NAVY CUT
Tobacco and Cigarettes

SHELL
CARS FOR HIRE

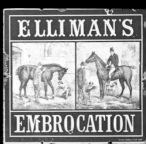
ELLIMAN'S
EMBROCATION

YOUR TOBACCONIST
sells

ZEBRA
Grate Polish

THE SMOKER'S MATCH
SWAN VESTAS
BRITISH MADE BY BRYANT & MAY

POWERFUL
PE&S
HUDSON'S SOAP
EASY AND SAFE

GUINNESS IS GOOD FOR YOU
GIVES YOU STRENGTH

.You know it by this.
"HIS MASTER'S VOICE."

STARTLING DISCOVERY
VENUS SOAP
SAVES RUBBING

SPILLERS
Cattle, Pig & Poultry Foods

MARTINI

VERMOUTH

BELGA

VANDER ELST

Mobiloil

VACUUM OIL COMPANY LTD

GUINNESS
is good for you

REDGATE SOLD HERE
Table Waters
Enjoyed the year round since 1878!

Rowntree's
PASTILLES

MORRIS
Sales and Service

"MATCHLESS"
METAL POLISH

Makers by Royal Warrant
JONES
SEWING
MACHINES
To Her Majesty the Queen

It pays to pay less and fit LISSEN
LISSEN
MICA PLUGS
GUARANTEED FOR ONE YEAR

ADKIN'S
NUT BROWN
TOBACCO

OGDEN'S
WALNUT
OGDEN'S
WALNUT PLUG
SLICED
PLUG

"ACE of SPADES"
SPECIAL BRAND
LUCAS'
SOLD HERE

Colman's
Starch

NECTAR
TEA

SMOKE
PLAYER'S
"AIRMAN"
TOBACCO

MAURETANIA

Drink
TIZER
The Appetizer

Coolness.
Fragrance.
A MEDIUM MIXTURE
"The Chairman"
R.J.LEA Ltd MANCHESTER
6d Per Oz.
Distinctive
Flavour.

HOLZAPFEL'S
COMPOSITIONS

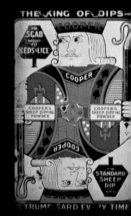

STRANGE'S A-1 CRYSTAL OIL

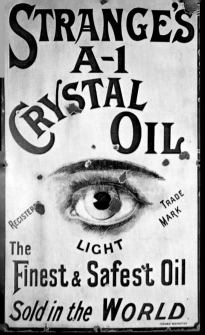

REGISTERED TRADE MARK

LIGHT

The Finest & Safest Oil Sold in the WORLD

TURF
TOP QUALITY CIGARETTES

DON'T BE MISLED !!!

DRINK "CAMP"
IT'S THE BEST

Sole Proprietors: R. PATERSON & SONS LTD. GLASGOW.

INGERSOLL

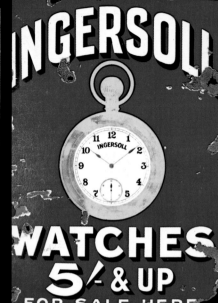

INGERSOLL

WATCHES 5/- & UP
FOR SALE HERE

OGDEN'S BATTLEAXE

OGDEN'S BATTLE AXE SLICED BAR

BATTLE AXE SLICED

BAR

BURMA SAUCE

THE ONLY "SAUCE" I DARE GIVE FATHER

GET YOUR
Player's Please
HERE

COLMAN'S
D.S.F.
MUSTARD

£1000 SUNLIGHT SOAP
GUARANTEE OF PURITY

THE ORIGINAL STURMEY-ARCHER 3 SPEED & TRICOASTER

WILLS'S FLAG

FLAG CIGARETTES

W.D. & H.O. WILLS

COOLIE CUT PLUG
FULL FLAVOUR   SWEET & LASTING

CIGARETTES

WILL'S'S

GOLD FLAKE
CIGARETTES
★ GOLD FLAKE ★
W.D.&H.O.WILLS.
BRISTOL & LONDON.

CIGARETTES
SOLD HERE.

BROOKE, BONDS' TEA.

SMOKE
CRAVEN "A"
WILL NOT AFFECT
YOUR THROAT

will
not
affect
your
throat

SMOKE
WALNUT
PLUG
"Sweet as a Nut"

WE SELL
ELEY
KYNOCH
CARTRIDGES

LYONS TEA

Drink
TIZER
The Appetizer

COLMAN'S
MUSTARD

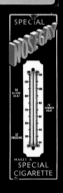

SPECIAL
NOSEGAY
98 BLOOD HEAT
76 SUMMER HEAT
32 FREEZING
MAKES A
SPECIAL
CIGARETTE

THOUSANDS IN USE
PETTER
OIL ENGINES
& ELECTRIC LIGHTING PLANTS
WORKS:- YEOVIL, ENGLAND.

HUNTLEY & PALMERS
GINGER NUTS
John Ginger
READING & LONDON,
ENGLAND.
MADE IN ENGLAND.

SWAN WHITE FLOATING SOAP
ABSOLUTELY PURE

GET

PRATT'S

HERE

Brilliant Economical
Lasting Easy
PELAW
LIQUID
METAL
POLISH

C.W.S. LIQUID
METAL POLISH
FOR ALL METALS
PELAW
SOLD BY ALL
CO-OPERATIVE SOCIETIES

THE "NUGGET"

TRADE MARK REGD.
WATERPROOF
BLACK POLISH
UNEQUALLED

TRADE MARK
REGIS TERED

FREE FROM ACID OF ANY DESCRIPTION.
PRESERVING LEATHER FROM CRACKING

FOR PATENT, GLACÉ KID, BOX
CALF AND OTHER LEATHERS

LONDON. S.E.

ASK FOR
PILLS
MADE BY
PARKINSONS

DELICIOUS
MAZAWATTEE
TEA

ADKIN'S

NUT BROWN

ADKIN & SONS EXTRA QUALITY
ADKIN & SONS EXTRA QUALITY

"NUT BROWN"
SOLD HERE

THE LEADING LINE.
TIP
TOP
TEA

THE HOP LEAF

57

An examination of the major design elements such as size, shape, colour and content, provides a clear insight into the developing taste of succeeding generations of advertisers.

Sizes ranged from as little as a few inches square, to composite giants covering areas in excess of forty square feet. An example of the former is Veritas Gas Mantles and of the latter Van Houten's Cocoa. However, the average size of signs was from three to four feet in height and width, with occasional long and narrow expanses of six or seven feet by a few inches. The factor determining this as an average size was generally the restriction of locations, as already indicated, and the majority of signs were to be found underneath shop windows. However, other locations on shops themselves, dictated different sizes and proportions such as shapes that would fit vertically on door frames and horizontally on counter fronts.

There were two main shape categories, those that were not based totally on the particular product being advertised and those cut out in the form of the product that the sign was advertising. Of the latter type, Nectar Tea was in the shape of a cup and saucer, Mobil and Shell Oils both took the form of cans and Mazawattee tea was delicately cut out around the saw-tooth shape of a tea leaf. Some shapes, though not made in the form of the product, were cut around intricate outlines. For examples, figures such as the Sunlight Soap boy offering a bag of £1,000 reward money perched on a bar of soap, or the man riding a Raleigh bicycle. Of the first category, apart from the normal rectangular shapes, other general shapes could be seen in the forms of ovals, circles,

triangles, lozenges, arrows, shields or a combination of these. Examples of these were: oval – Nestlé's Milk, circle – Lyons' Cakes, Lucas Batteries, triangle – BP and Shell Oils, lozenge – Renault Cars, John Bull Tyres, arrow – Shell Petrol, shield – BSA Bicycles, Walter Willson's Stores, combined shapes – Craven 'A' Cigarettes, Karpol Car Polish, Morris Cars. It must be added that many signs were double-sided, projecting from the wall and attached by brackets, chains and hooks. This method not only doubled the visual effectiveness of the sign, but also added to its strength and stability, since there was thick enamel on both sides. Normally only a thin layer of counter-enamel was put on the reverse side during processing. Examples of these double-sided signs are: Royal Daylight Lamp Oil, Will's Star Cigarettes, Lyons' Cakes, Shell Lubricating Oil, Hay's Cleaners, Churchman's Number 1 Cigarettes. Some, like Lyons' Cakes signs had elaborate wrought iron frames. Domed or bulbous signs used for early Lyon's Tea and late John Bull Tyres were never popular in this country, but they were used extensively on the continent, in fact, the original Lyon's tea signs were ordered from Germany. Another example of this type is the Fry's Cocoa Shield.

For the convenience of the customer, stores would often provide chairs to sit on while they gave their orders and often these chairs were issued to the shopkeeper by the advertisers who had had inserted into the back of the chair an enamel plaque such as Watson's Matchless Cleanser or Venus Soap. Other three-dimensional signs took the form of 'A' shaped sandwich boards which stood on the pavement outside shops and were portable and free-standing. Companies using this method were Palethorpes, who had a set with sausages on one side and a pork pie on the other and Lyon's who had a fruit pie on one side and an ice cream advertisement on the other.

There were also enamel plated vending machines attached to walls, advertising the contents, such as chocolate, mints, razor blades and cigarettes. Examples have been found of ash trays, dog water bowls, scales, pub checker-boards, shoe-shine stands, trays, wall clocks and shop opening time indicators, all advertising products on their enamelled surfaces.

59

Unframed signs were usually large and found at a high level above a fascia or on gable ends. Framed signs normally consisted of a plate, slotted or screwed into a wooden moulding, sometimes strengthened with angle plates on the back at each corner. On long signs it was often necessary to brace these with cross stretchers. The whole sign and frame was fixed to the building fabric by means of drilled plates or alternatively screwed directly through the face of the frame. The techniques of fixing varied from one sign manufacturer to another, but in most cases the fixings were supplied painted gloss black. However, most framing, painted or otherwise, naturally rots with the passing of the years. Unframed signs were usually attached by means of either screws and lead washers, through ready-made holes in the sign, or masonry nails with flat heads, retaining the sign where the holes were either inappropriate or not included. Most signs, from a few inches square up to six feet square, had between two and eight screws or nails per side. Pointing was occasionally used as an additional means of support on uneven wall surfaces. These unframed signs tended to corrode faster at the fixing points due to the total exposure of the edges and back. In Germany in 1949, a method of avoiding surface corrosion through damaged screwholes was patented. This comprised slightly extended corners springing from either shallowly rebated edges, or from concave-surfaced plates. Further protection was afforded by placing maleable washers over the fixing holes. Points of corrosion also arose from the stone and air gun attacks of generations of youths.

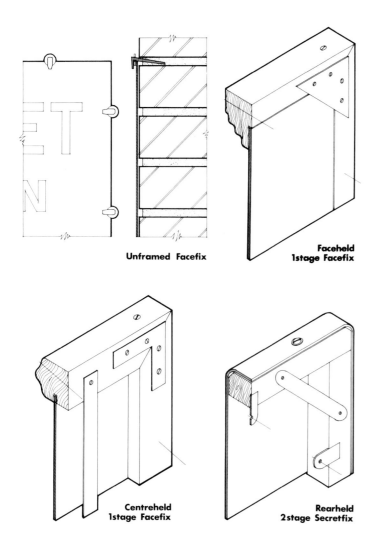

Unframed Facefix

Faceheld 1stage Facefix

Centreheld 1stage Facefix

Rearheld 2stage Secretfix

The area of heat-fused glass from which the surface of an enamelled sign is created has certain textural and visual qualities peculiar to the enamel medium, which are particularly pleasing and in sharp contrast to the surface of other pictorial media such as paint, wood, paper or plaster. Each colour is individually applied – on top of or slightly overlapping the edge of the one below – and each has its own distinct edge separating it from its neighbours. A meniscus is formed during the period when the glass is molten and remains on the edge of each layer and this can best be appreciated by running the fingers gently over the undulating surface. Some manufacturing methods created a more exaggerated manifestaiton of this effect, so that the surface of the Ogden's series, with blue background and red and yellow lettering, is particularly bumpy. The play of light over the surface is broken up into variegated planes and facets, which are enhanced if the sign is in good condition and carefully polished. Enamel is semi-transparent and highly reflective and can produce colours and tones of great richness and depth. The frequent use of bright primary colours and the sparkling bright surface effect that the best designs afford, linked with the similarity in materials used in fine and applied art enamelling, suggest the simile 'street jewellery'.

One of the most appealing characteristics of enamelled advertising signs, from a pure design point of view, and from an historical aspect, is their embodiment of a variety of different typestyles together on one sign. Each one was chosen to perform its own eye-catching function.

It is interesting to note the use of free-flowing lettering for Rowntree's pastilles, the italic script of Veritas Mantles and the soft, three-dimensional forms used on Player's Airman and Camp Coffee. Our eyes pass on to the harder forms of block shadows on the serif letters of Shell and to the sans-serif of Tizer and outline on Raleigh.

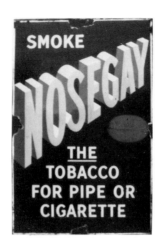

All these typestyles and their variants help us to date signs as well as giving each its peculiar individuality. Several signs illustrated show the use of particularly fashionable typefaces of certain eras. For example the Art Nouveau period is represented by the ornate lettering of Swan Ink, Lucas Spades, Nectar Tea and Bovril.

Another interesting aspect of letter forms on signs is the use of a number of different styles on the same plate. Palethorpes use three completely different faces in as many words. Similar richness of styles can be noted on P. & R. Hay Dyers & Cleaners, and on the brown background of Fry's Chocolate.

The Foremost Humorous Journal of the World

PUNCH

THREE PENCE

"Its Columns Sparkle with Wit and Wisdom"

The QUEEN

THE LADY'S NEWSPAPER

& COURT CHRONICLE

EVERY FRIDAY
Price 6d.

The Sketch

6D-

WEEKLY.

WEDNESDAY

OFFICE
198 STRAND

FIELD

THE FARM   THE GARDEN

THE COUNTRY
GENTLEMAN'S NEWSPAPER

EVERY SATURDAY.
Price 6d.

½d.   ½d.

STAR

LARGEST CIRCULATION
OF ANY
EVENING PAPER

PEARSON'S WEEKLY

ONE   PENNY

THE SMALLHOLDER

EVERY THURSDAY

The earliest method of applying a pattern to the iron plate was by the elaborate and skilful use of stencilling. Where more than two colours were used, a considerable feeling for the essence of the medium was required of the designer. To build up stylised images by means of multiple stencil overlays, without the use of half-tones, was a highly skilled job and required a bold sense of pattern and tonal appreciation, for a successful result to be achieved. With the introduction of lithographic techniques as an imitation of and in parallel use by other poster-type advertising media, a basic honesty and integrity in the medium was lost. Even when the image was produced by transfer or litho printing, the major colour areas and the larger lettering were usually stencilled, e.g. the rare early photograph and stencilled Royal Daylight American Lamp Oil. But a comparison between an image produced exclusively by stencilling – Champion Norfolk Boots – and one made by borrowing a printing medium – Holzapfels Compositions – which is a monochrome lithograph tinted with stencilled areas of colour, indicates the purity of the one and the decadence of the other. The intrinsic quality of the enamel texture is still retained in both cases, making both varieties visually and technically acceptable to the collector.

Screen printing was first used by the National Sign Company, circa 1923, and here the effect of stencilling, litho and photography could be combined in one process, e.g. Spillers Balanced Rations, made in Newcastle. Nearly all the modern enamel signs are made using the screen printing process and applied on steel. A direct comparison between an original sign of the early period and a modern reproduction gives a clear demonstration of the difference in quality and finish between the old process and the new. A certain clarity and luminosity typifies the originals, whereas the modern versions tend towards the clinical and meagre.

Collecting, Conservation, Restoration

Not all collectors of enamels concentrate exclusively on signs. Frequently a sprinkling of enamel advertisements will usefully augment another interest. Thus, for example, for some people the prime consideration is the product shown on the sign. Motoring enthusiasts have dozens of examples to choose from, though not many show actual vehicles. Sun Motor Insurance is one and another is a fine image of Malcolm Campbell and the Bluebird on a Castrol sign. In other spheres of interest, specialists will consider signs illustrating bottles, packages and tins to have premium value. Also included in the latter category are those signs displaying out-dated prices for products, e.g. Whitbread Pale Ale 2/6 a dozen, and out-moded trading slogans.

Specialisation by the collector in certain product types or brands will affect the value of signs. The parallel trends in ephemera collecting, such as labels, bottles and packaging often influence this. The signs featuring bottles – Dartnell's Ginger Beer, Green & Leddicott's with Zeppelin bottles and Brighton Pier, soap and cigarette packs – Hudson's, Sunlight, Woodbine – or labels and trademarks – Guinness and Gossages – will have special preference and enhanced value for collectors specialising in examples of these items themselves. Similarly, certain non-advertising enamel signs hold special interest for collectors of railway or military ephemera, such as station nameplates or recruiting notices.

Because of their small size, and the consequent ease of display, fingerplates are particularly collectable. They occur in various materials (ceramic, glass, brass and tin), but most advertising and match-striking fingerplates are in enamel. Advertising fingerplates were usually used on the entrance doors to shops, and can still be found in older properties (although now usually under layers of paint). Some of the more commonly encountered advertisers are Barbers (tea), Carreras (cigarettes), Thomsons (dyes), Ogdens, Colman's, Hudsons, Shell

and Players. Often fingerplates on the inside of shop doors would incorporate match-strikers (Morris's, Players, Spratts and Coca-Cola). In the same collectable category of miniature size, are counter front signs, though these come in a slender horizontal format.

Since no sign is more than a century old, and most signs of the last thirty years are not much admired by collectors, the parameters of vintage for individual signs will fall into the last two decades of the nineteenth century and the first of the twentieth. All signs thereafter may be classified as modern. Victorian objects of all sorts have a special prestige for collectors of advertising ephemera and in this respect, enamels are no exception. However, apart from this consideration, the relative age of a sign is not a strong determining factor. Some designs remained in production for decades and as such are difficult to date precisely. But, as the stylisation of typefaces and imagery, typical of Victorian and Edwardian manufacture often finds a more appreciative audience than those of the inter-war years, so these older examples (provided they combine some of the appropriate qualities of bold and variegated typestyles, quaint imagery or illustration, an out-moded message or a product with bright colours and good condition) tend to be the most desirable and hardest to obtain. It is now extremely rare to find this type of sign *in situ*. Those that do survive are usually in collections already or turn up in the storage areas of old business premises. Signs with similar visual qualities, but of more recent date, will fetch comparable prices. Again the desirability of signs with less visual richness i.e. lettering only, a few colours and no image, depends on content rather than on age. Only if a date is prominent on the design e.g. Sunlight Soap Highest Award Chicago 1893, or a reference to a monarch (ibid.) will the value of the piece be influenced. Sometimes a date code can be discerned on the sign, usually on the lower righthand corner, in the form of 7:10, indicating July 1910 and occasionally on the back of

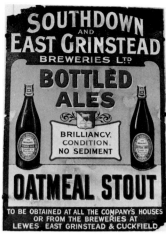

the sign. Age can also be determined by the back coating being either grey swilled or black, as described in the chapter on technical processes.

How do collectors come by their signs: There is, as with any collectable, a floating market exchange between dealers and collectors, in antique shops, flea markets, auto jumbles and especially from private specialist dealers. However, most big collections are created by the patient scouring and searching of likely and unlikely locations.

In the normal course of events the locations and usefulness of these old advertisements vanish with time and custom. Thousands of miles of terraced streets, which once served as display areas for a thousand or more signs, have disappeared since the War years. Sometimes these signs were systematically removed by their original distributors, but more often they were simply abandoned. The big tobacco firms and petrol companies were particularly active in pursuing a policy of constant renewal of their advertising images, and consequently they replaced and updated their signs. The remainder were left, unmaintained, on the walls. From this abandoned wealth of material only a small proportion has survived and been preserved in good condition, either accidentally or by intent, thus some examples are quite rare now and are sought after by collectors and museums.

The factors determining the collectability of signs and their consequent monetary value, vary according to circumstances. With a mass-produced object such as a sign, rarity is hard to establish, as occasionally large *câches* of particular signs are discovered in warehouses where they have lain, well preserved, for years. Even under the quite arduous conditions of chance survival, such as re-use for building material in a garden shed or compost heap, or buried in a rubbish dump, the enamelled iron sign can survive remarkably well.

One factor which for most serious collectors underlies all others, is the condition of the sign. A mint

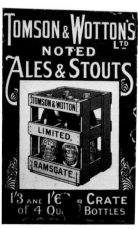

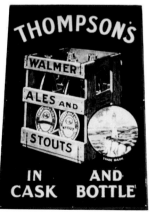

sign, or one with minimal damage such as flaking of the enamel around the screw holes, or slight chipping or corrosion around the edges, is highly prized, as with all collectables. But if it is visually unexciting, even a mint condition sign is not desirable. The most perfectly preserved old specimen of a two-colour, simply-lettered and phrased sign, with no illustration and advertising a dull and mundane product, will not enhance a collection. It is easy to understand the value put on illustrations, and of conveniently small size, say 3' square or smaller, lots of bright colour, or lettering that is complex, ornate or stylised.

Other desirable qualities in enamelled advertisements are more peculiar to this medium and are not evident in other poster-type advertising. The shaped sign, either geometrically varying from the rectangle or made in a figurative shape for outside use, in practical terms, possible only in enamelled metal, as are opening and closing time clocks, front-of-counter dog's drinking bowls and the backs of chairs for waiting customers. Wooden, card and ceramic alternatives did not have the permanence or brightness of enamelled iron and only the introduction of plastics put an end to the dominance of enamel for these trade gimmicks. Among the most desirable of these shaped signs are the cut-out, projecting, double-sided signs, two examples of which are a pair of hands holding a bottle of 1d Monsters Pop and a fleecy ram extolling the virtues of Cooper's Sheep Dip. The collector can enrich the range of his collection

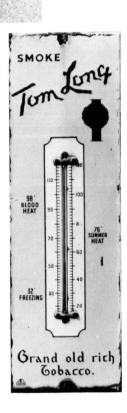

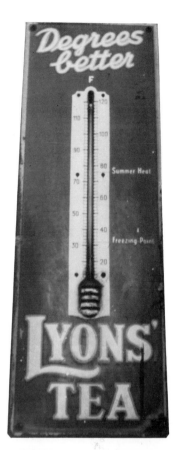

by finding enamelled vending machines, door finger plates, thermometers and barometers. Classics of the silhouette cut-out are illustrated in the colour plates. The Sunlight Soap boy, the Mazawattee Tea leaf are there, but not, unfortunately, the delightful Fremlin's lager elephant.

The main location of *in situ* signs is still the shop front in the older quarters of industrial cities, either on existing traders' premises or on derelict buildings and gable ends. Generally permission is easily gained from shopkeepers, landlords and estate agents, or original manufacturers for the removal of the signs. It is advisable to offer to undertake remedial work for unsightly or inconvenient gaps left by their removal. This may involve painting, pointing and re-timbering, but for a prize specimen the effort involved is well rewarded.

Removal of the sign itself is a skill only acquired through experience. As the iron/steel and glass of the artefact are brittle and at the same time strong and heavy, controlled strength is required and to climb 40 feet up a ladder means a strong head for heights too!

Equipment required for on site collecting:

Van with roof rack and extendable ladders
Saws for metal and wood
Brace and bit with metal drills to drill out screws
Heavy duty screwdriver
Crowbar and/or levers
Hammer, pincers, pliers
Strong gloves
Penetrating oil and sharp eyes

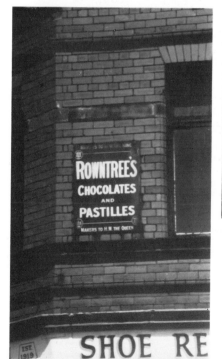

York Castle Museum.

In the conservation of inner city areas, architects are constantly faced with old forms of advertising on shop fronts, interiors, hoardings and gable ends, which are not always considered worthy of restoration along with the rest of the building. The most common external advertising of any great age surviving today is the enamelled iron sign. These brilliantly coloured signs have endured more than other types of ephemeral advertising because of their strong construction materials and permanent means of attachment. Unfortunately, in new building work on existing property, such signs are far too often relegated to the contractor's waste skip and thus lost to future generations. Enamel signs were used by advertisers because of their special permanence, and thus embody a strong historical continuity. Their shape was frequently dictated by the facade details of the shop and thus became a decorative architectural feature in much the same way as glazed ceramic tiles and engraved glass windows. They survive as historical documents. If the sign is to be conserved *in situ* then it should be removed for inspection and cleaning. The back will usually have corrosion streaks which can be scoured off and sealed with car underseal or polyurethane varnish.

If there is a frame, it will probably be rotted and if so it should be replaced. Even if sound or replaced, it should be treated to inhibit future decay. The front surface of the plate can be cleaned as described in the following section and returned to its fixing.

Although most shop fascias on the street are now renovated and modernised, leaving no room for or trace of enamels, a few museums of bygones (p. 101) have on display reconstructions of street scenes of earlier times which include many examples of such signs. There are also abundant photographic records of signs *in situ* and elsewhere to which the enthusiast can refer. To see enamel signs *in situ* in environments similar to those in which they were originally used, it is now necessary to visit industrial, vernacular and steam railway museums, where enamel signs are often used to lend an 'authentic' period ambience.

Beamish North of England Open Air Museum.

When a sign is collected it should be checked over for rust damage on the front and back. If it has survived with the enamel intact, a very rare occurence, then no action need be taken apart from cleaning with the appropriate cleanser, i.e. scouring paste and warm water applied with a cloth for mild surface dirt, or wire wool and scouring powder, with frequent sluicings to shift really ingrained dirt. Care must be taken with delicate transfer and lithographed areas, and with certain black lettering and outline overlays. Rusted areas should be cleaned with a rust removing chemical agent, steel wool or emery and immediately sealed or treated with oil, anti-rust paint or underseal. Broken and chipped enamel cannot be satisfactorily replaced, except in small areas on a good metal surface, but even so the process requires complex equipment and technical skill. A method of replacing missing metal and enamel has been devised, using fibreglass and resin or the plastic padding normally used for car body repairs, and painted with enamel colours. Only expert manipulation of these materials yields agreeable results, so that in most cases of surface damage, the scars are best left undisguised and regarded with pleasure as the patina peculiarly associated with the medium. The construction of a wooden frame on which to screw the signs will usually be beneficial, in that a means of attachment to the wall is provided that does not involve danger to the enamel surface caused by repeated screw pressure or hammer blows. The plate is kept rigid and thus free from the splintering caused by bending and torque.

Restoration technique:

1. After thorough cleaning and de-rusting make sure the sign is rigid and flat by fixing with round-headed screws to a wooden frame. Lead or nylon washers may be introduced between the screw head and the enamel to avoid crushing the surface.
2. Back holes with aluminium mesh and resin. A greased card held to the enamel surface will keep bleed-through-resin to the correct level.
3. Fill the hole to the level of the enamel surface, repeatedly scraping it down rather than sanding, to keep the surface smooth and to avoid scratching the enamel.
4. Lightly paint with enamel paint, avoiding brush marks. Air brushing achieves best results.

NB. Painting in a dust-free atmosphere prevents a grainy texture. Blues are the hardest colours to match.
Sometimes a white undercoat will help.
All signs benefit from a vigorous wax polishing.

Burning paint off a sign

For the social historian the advent of mass advertising serves as an invaluable window through which the life of the late nineteenth century and early twentieth century can be viewed. For earlier periods we are dependent for such insights on those few buildings and cultural and domestic relics that have survived, and which generally reflect the life of only a small section of society.

Early mass advertising, of which the enamel sign is a significant and well preserved part, reflects the needs, desires, and requirements of a large section of industrial society, in particular the working and lower middle classes. It is a primary source of evidence of the fact that by the 1890s these sections of the populace were forming a significantly consumer based society, with an appreciable amount of disposable income. Various products which before the era of mass industrial production would have been luxury products, were now within the grasp of a large section of society. Raleigh, the all steel bicycle, Singer sewing machines, Petter's Oil engines for electric lighting plants are just a few examples of this. Increasing literacy is reflected, not only by the increasing use of the written word in advertising, but also by signs advertising writing materials such as Swan and Stephens inks and MacNiven and Cameron's pens. Increased awareness of hygiene and cleanliness is seen in the emphasis on soap advertisements, and improved conditions of comfort are indicated by the implied ability to purchase carpets – Chiver's carpet soap. Captured in its infancy is that product which so perfectly symbolises the age of mass production and popular affluence – the motor car – Morris, Sun Insurance and petrol.

The current face of advertising is so quickly outdated and superseded that we are accustomed to constant novelty in the medium. Advertising forms, too, are ephemeral. Thus, when a person who has been aware of consumer marketing campaigns for several decades is confronted with an example of advertising in a form that has long since vanished it is often with a feeling of friendly familiarity, as that of meeting a long-lost school chum for the first time in many years, that he will recognise and appreciate the old advertisement.

This syndrome is particularly true of the enamelled iron sign, since when they were first introduced, they remained in being for long periods and became landmarks in a local area. 'Turn right at the church and left at the Woodbine sign' must have been an almost natural instruction at one time. The familiarity and the association of the sign with the products they advertised and the evocation of using these products, raises a wave of nostalgia and sentimental association in the minds of those able to remember enamel signs as an everyday feature of their environment. A packet of Hudson's soap powder may well spark off a recall of washday, with all the associations of the smell of clothes in hot soap water, the regular sloshing of a dolly stick in the washing and the noisy gossip and clamour of housewives at the wash house and mangling shop. Who, even now, can remain unmoved by the allure of Tizer the Appetizer (and those summers that always seemed far longer and hotter) and Palethorpe's sausages, when due to the prevalence of their respective advertising campaigns these products' trade-names have become synonymous with the products themselves? Fry's Five Boys chocolate is still remembered vividly by the immediate post war generation and the architypal symbols of the boy's face in different moods still raises delighted grins, even though the Pavlovian association with mouth-watering chocolate can only lead to desperation since the product is no longer available and whether true or false didn't everything taste that much better then! So it is with much of the produce advertised on the signs. Many companies still thrive who used the medium to promote their goods and are prime users of magazine advertising space and television time. Many are now as defunct as the medium itself. It may lie with the present generation, with its championship of conservation and non-expendability to resurrect the enamel sign as a tree-saving, environment enhancing form of advertisement, with built in non-obsolescence, but that is a perhaps wistful thought, too optimistic to entertain seriously.

QUALITY & STRENGTH

Hercules CYCLES

ΤΑ ΚΥΝΗΓΕΤΙΚΑ ΟΠΛΑ ΠΙΠΕΡ ΕΙΝΑΙ ΤΑ ΚΑΛΛΙΤΕΡΑ

Fusil Bayard

MARQUE DÉPOSÉE
BAYARD

Fusil Diane

ΖΗΤΕΙΤΕ ΤΟ ΑΝΩ ΣΗΜΑ ΤΟΥ ΕΡΓΟΣΤΑΣΙΟΥ

Rudge-Whitworth
Britain's Best Bicycle

A GREAT BICYCLE WITH A GREAT REPUTATION

£5 TO £15

COVENTRY

WORKS AND HEAD OFFICES

BRISTOL
17 QUEENS ROAD

PRICES NEW PATENT NIGHT LIGHTS

PRICES CHILDS NIGHT LIGHTS
LONDON & LIVERPOOL

BOSCH
MAGNETOS
AND ACCESSORIES

RUBEROID

THE WORLD'S BEST

ROOFING

Remington
means TYPEWRITER

AGENT FOR THE
'FRAM' REGD
REAL GERMAN HOLLOW GROUND RAZOR

PRICE 4/6 EACH

NEVER REQUIRES GRINDING

FIRST FOR QUALITY
LAST FOR PRICE.

NEW HUDSON CYCLES

THE WORLDS BEST VALUE

NEW HUDSON CYCLE CO LIMITED BIRMINGHAM

EASY TERMS

6.12 OR 18 MONTHS.

RIDE A
RALEIGH
THE ALL-STEEL BICYCLE

INVALID CHAIRS
FOR SALE or HIRE

WRITE FOR CATALOGUES

CHAPLIN & CO.
REMOVALS & WAREHOUSING

ROAD RAIL OR SEA

REMOVALS WAREHOUSING ESTIMATES FREE

TEL No 247

CHAPLIN & CO. 12. GROVE ROAD FOLKESTONE

12. GROVE ROAD. FOLKESTONE.

L & C. HARDTMUTH'S
"KOH-I-NOOR"
PENCILS
MADE IN 17 DEGREES
FOR ALL PURPOSES

CRIDDLE & SMITH

ART FURNITURE, CARPETS, CURTAINS, DECORATIONS, BEDSTEADS, BEDDING.

FURNITURE REMOVED & WAREHOUSED

CRIDDLE & SMITH.
TRURO
COMPLETE HOUSE FURNISHERS
TRURO & PENZANCE No 4

FURNITURE REMOVERS. ESTIMATES FREE. DRY ROOMS FOR WAREHOUSING.

HOUSE & ESTATE AGENTS. REGISTERS ISSUED MONTHLY.

TRURO & PENZANCE

GOODLASS, WALL & CO. L TD

SOLE MAKERS OF SWANSDOWN ENAMEL

FAST RED
PAINTS THE TOWN

SPECIALISTS TO THE SHIPPING TRADE

MANUFACTURERS TRADE MARK OF HIGHEST GRADE

PAINTS, COLOURS & VARNISH
42 & 44 SEEL ST
LIVERPOOL

BRITISH MADE.
COGSHULTZ AMMUNITION
SOLD HERE

PICKFORD & CO

BOOKING OFFICE FOR SUBURBAN

LONDON
AND
UNIVERSAL PARCEL EXPRESS

CHIEF OFFICE CASTLE ST.

MATCHLESS
METAL POLISH

Manufacturers past and present, home and abroad

Much of the historical and technical data for this book is based on information supplied by Ivor Beard a director of the late Patent Enamel Co., he being the last of three generations of his family to work there, his grandfather having been a co-founder with Benjamin Baugh. He recalls the hey-day of enamel sign manufacture during his boyhood and how he watched with regret, the decline in demand which he claims coincided particularly with the end of railway expansion. He recalls several attempts to revitalise the industry by mergers between companies, notably the big three – Patent, Chromographic of Wolverhampton and Imperial of Birmingham. But these measures came to nothing with the onset of the Depression years. Further problems and crises during and after the War included an acute steel shortage, when rationing precluded the use of this vital commodity for advertising purposes. Aluminium which was cheaper and more readily accessible, served as an alternative for a while, but true enamelled iron sign making in the grand scale was gone forever by the 1950s. Also at this time many of the old enamel sign plants were taken over by manufacturers of baths and cookers for in-factory enamelling facilities. Amalgamations and single company franchise of petrol stations and breweries meant that fewer types of signs were needed and thus orders were denied to the industry. Simultaneously trade was being constantly lost as small businesses, such as ice-cream makers, bakers and soft drinks manufacturers declined in the face of competition from the large combines. The demise of the small firm and the development of chain stores – although some of these like Walter Willson used enamels to advertise – meant that the small local enamelling firms also went out of business for lack of custom.

One firm which has survived all these crises from its foundation by exiled Frenchman, Charles Garnier in 1898, until the present day, is Garnier Signs of Willesden

Period Swedish design studio

Green, London and an example of their work is used on the cover of this book. Their factory has always been at Willesden, but up to 1941 their registered office and showrooms were at Farringdon Street, until these were destroyed by enemy action. The Farringdon Street address can be seen on this Lloyd's News sign of circa 1918–23. Other manufacturers who used Garnier signs over the years included Nugget Polishes, Van Houten's Cocoa and Nosegay Tobacco (p. 94). Garnier's made the still familiar, but fast-disappearing, stamped-out enamelled copper letters, which are glued with mastic varnish to shop windows and which advertise Typhoo Tea and Cadbury's. These letters were devised originally by yet another extant firm – Burnham's (Onyx) Ltd. who had a large contract to supply advertising signs for Fry's.

A very extensive use of signs was to plate complete shop fronts in a uniform 'house style'. Garnier's supplied signs for this purpose to Sunlight and Western Laundries and for Boar's Head Tobacco and also to various small merchants and tradesmen who used enamelled plates to cover their trading carts, on fronts, sides and tailboards. Patent Enamel followed a similar course by supplying such overall sign coverage for shop fascias to advertise 'The News of the World' – a blue plate with white lettering, installed as late as the 1960s – and Ogden's. The Ogden's panels were devised to imitate wood-graining for oak, walnut and mahogany finishes and bore not only the names of cigarette and tobacco brands, but also, like those for 'The News of the World', the name of the shop proprietor.

Garnier's motto 'Nothing too large and nothing too small' is illustrated by an anecdote recalled by the staff there. Sometimes a situation would arise when, for instance, 160' long panels in sections were being processed at the same time as 100,000 2"×2" licence plates. The biggest signs for advertising display had to be laid out on the road to ensure that all the panels matched up and that the sign was spelt correctly!

Over the last decade, Garnier's has absorbed the work and engaged staff of companies which closed down, namely Chromographic of Wolverhampton and James Bruton and Son Ltd of Palmers Green, both of which were of the same vintage as Garniers.

Garnier's is now the largest manufacturer of reproduction signs marketed both in this country and abroad.

A complete review of sign manufacture worldwide has yet to be undertaken, but in recent years research in Europe has led to several excellent books on the history of Continental enamel advertising. It is from these, and from information supplied by European collectors and manufacturers that the following resumé is drawn.

Belgium
L'émaillerie Belge, the earliest Belgian company to produce enamel signs, has been doing so since 1923. Their current range includes decorative enamel panels, one series of which features designs by Hergé the creator of Tin Tin.

However the earliest dateable Belgian enamel (1925), is by the Koekelburg Company, and advertises the Petre de Vos brewery. Its typeface is typical Art Deco.

Most Belgian-origin enamels advertise beers, tobaccos and confectionery. Examples include a c.1930 double-sider for Araks cigarettes (Koekelberg), a shaped beer glass advertising Haecht beer (1949, Email-Chrom, Weerde, Mechelen), and many signs for Belga cigarettes and Beukelaar cocoa confectioners, both pre and post WW II.

France
When Jules Cherét introduced chromolithographic printing techniques to French poster makers in 1866, he soon became known as the 'Fragonard of the Pallisades'. With significant artists like Toulouse-Lautrec and Mucha taking to this medium, and establishing a tradition of excellence in advertising design in the 1880s, it is hardly surprising that early French enamels using chromolithography are of a standard unsurpassed since.

Hand printed porcelain enamel OLD ADVERTISEMENTS

The Street Jewellery of Yesteryear.

A combination of old skills and processes by a Company established in 1898 which produced some of the very collectable originals.

Bold — Colourful — Attractive

Miniatures size 50mm x 65mm are also made — refer to price list for wordings offered.

PERSIL — HUNTLEY & PALMERS — MICHELIN DISCONTINUED

Garnier & Co. Ltd., 37 Strode Road, Willesden Green, London NW10 2NP. Tel: 01-459 0152

Two of the best from the 'belle époque', c.1895, both feature little girls, one of whom advertises Menier chocolate by scribbling the slogan 'Beware of Imitations' on a wall, the other – for Maggi soup cubes – actually has the girl holding an enamel sign advertising Maggi in her hands. French enamels between the Wars really took advantage of the proto hi-tech lines of Art Deco, and promoted products such as Pfaff sewing machines, Tungstrem radio valves, and Desmarais motor oil, among many others to excellent effect. However, the signs for Nicolas, St. Raphael, Ricard and Byrrh may be more familiar examples of this type, exploiting uncompromisingly the bright bold patchwork of pure enamel colour fields. The production of enamels in France reached its height in the 20s and 30s, causing shopfronts to be astonishing mosaics of enamel signs.

Legislation does not seem to have been as draconian in France as it was in Germany. While apparently natural 'good taste' kept the centre of Paris clear of signs except on the 'colonnes Morice' and in the Metro, the suburbs teemed with signs, both in Paris and in all the large, mainly industrial towns of the North. Rural and mountain areas and villages remained fairly clear of signs.

French product manufacturers made contracts with shop-keepers in the inter-War years, to the effect that they would provide signs, but that the maintenance of them should then become the responsibility of the retailers.

French enamelling works abounded from the 1880's onwards, but none of them specialised in advertising signs, until l'Emaillerie Alsacienne was opened in Strasbourg in 1927. A classic sign from that factory is Engrais d'Auby, of 1929, featuring a smiling farm lad carrying an outsize parsnip on his back. Other French makers include Ed. Jean, E.A.S., l'Emaillerie du Loiret, and l'Emaillerie du Rhone, however many signs used in France were manufactured in Belgium.

Germany

The process of enamelling iron for the production of items of domestic use was originally suggested in 1761 by Heinrich Gottlieb von Justi, and after much experimentation during the following century, manufacturers were able to enjoy the thriving production of enamelled iron artefacts (as witnessed by Benjamin Baugh) by the 1860s.

The earliest firms in Germany to specialise in the production of enamel advertising signs were Schulze & Wehrmann (1893), C. Robert Dold (1894), Gottfried Dichanz (1895) and Otto Leroi (Frankfurt) (1897). As a result of the increased use of enamel advertising, road and traffic signs etc., many factories were established just before, and especially after WW I. Prior to WW II there were over 300 enamel works, 30 of them specialising in the production of advertisements. Barely a dozen firms now produce them.

Ernst Litfass, a Berlin printer, introduced the street advertising column in about 1850. Whether enamel signs were made to fit these is not stated in the literature, but apparently advertising signs and posters of all kinds had proliferated so much by 1907, that the police authorities of many German states including Prussia, Saxony and Bavaria were given special powers to license the display of signs, and to oblige advertisers to remove signs placed in designated areas of architectural or aesthetic beauty or historical significance. This curbing by police of advertising freedom so worried the profession, that an

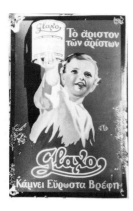

'Organisation of Advertising Producers and Users' was formed in 1910, with the intention of reforming advertising standards by self-determination, thus avoiding the imposition of regulations by external legal authorities.

The chief users of enamels in Germany were Maggi, Suchard, Persil, and Palmin. For German enamel sign enthusiasts one of the most celebrated advertising campaigns was mounted by Henkel of Dusseldorf for Persil, and featured the Persil White woman, designed by Berlin poster artist Kurt Heilighstadte in 1922.

Greece

According to Leo Lambert and Spyros Kypriotis, Greece's chief enamophiles, enamel signs did not 'catch on' too well in that country, despite some lovely designs being produced. Apparently most were immediately junked, or recycled by Greek shop-keepers. The manufacturers in Greece have kept no records of production, but to judge by the remaining examples many were used to advertise childrens' milk products, beer, toothpaste and weapons. Most date from the 1930s and slightly before. Evidently many were produced in other parts of Europe, and had Greek language slogans printed on images which were used by the same advertisers as far away as Sweden.

Holland

There is presently only one Dutch enamel factory, known as B.V. United Dutch Enamel Factories, 'Longcat'. It was formed by mergers in the 1920s. The first development of a specialist enamel department was in the tin factory founded and owned by Wood and Schraap (founded 1917). In 1921 this firm expanded by buying an enamelling firm in Bussen, owned by Keizer and Bottema. Langcat has an archive in the form of a sample room at its factory in Bussen.

Sweden

Sweden's first enamel works was Ankarsrum's, founded in Smaland in 1884, and first producing enamel signs in August 1890, under the direction of a German craftsman called Christian Lehman from Baden. Signs for all functions, including advertising, were produced.

According to a catalogue of 1900, prices were set by size and the amount of text. Black or blue and white were at basic cost. The addition of red or yellow increased the cost by 20%.

The Olofstrom works opened in 1887, followed by the Eskilsuma works in 1893. Two other firms founded in the 1890s, Svea's and Sprakered's survive into the 1980s, now producing hand-made enamel signs.

Sweden's foremost enamel buff is Olle Nessle, who with Birgitta Conradson wrote 'Svenska Skyltar', and popularised the preservation, collection and museum display of enamels in the late 1970s, after a decade of research.

Other countries

Little has as yet been forthcoming about enamel signs in other parts of the world, but Mike Cavanagh of Bourton-on-the-Water Motor Museum, has observed locally produced signs in South Africa, mainly devoted to mining, and several Australian and New Zealand collectors have reported signs native to their countries. From the U.S.A. the only significant companies to have employed enamel as an advertising medium seem to be Ford, Chrysler and Coca Cola.

ENAMELLED IRON PLATES
SINGLE-SIDED. DOUBLE-SIDED. FLAT. BENT. SHAPED
IN ANY SIZE —— IN ANY QUANTITY

HOT WATER
NIGHT OR DAY
WITHOUT THE USE OF COAL

From ALL PARTICULARS
THE GAS LIGHT & COKE Co.
Horseferry Rd.
WESTMINSTER S.W

Actual Size 2 ft. × 1¼ ft.

Actual Size 9 in. × 11 in.

GARNIER & Co LTD
ENAMELLED PLATES
NOTHING TOO LARGE! NOTHING TOO SMALL!!
FOR ANY & EVERY PURPOSE
MANUFACTURERS

BUDDLES
UNDERTAKER
FRONT STREET, NEWBIGGIN.
BOARD KEPT HERE

Actual Size 2½ ft. × 2 ft.

Schweppes
SODA WATER

Actual Size 2 ft. × 2 ft

MEMBER OF THE LOCAL
LICENSED VICTUALLERS
AND
BEER RETAILERS
ASSOCIATION

Actual Size 13 in. × 11 in.

THE RISING SUN

For Roadside Inns.

MOTORISTS BEWARE OF TRAPS & SPEED LIMITS THROUGH REIGATE
28 MILES TO HATCHETTS
PICCADILLY. W.
ACKNOWLEDGED TO BE
THE BEST & MOST SELECT MODERATE PRICED
RESTAURANT & GRILL ROOM
IN LONDON
A la carte - a speciality
Table d'hôte Lunch 2/6, Dinner 3/6, Supper 2/6.
MUSIC

FIELD PLATES—Actual Size 12 ft. × 8 ft.

Daily Mail
LARGEST CIRCULATION

Actual Size 4 ft. 6 in. × 2 ft. 10 in.

PLATES SUITABLE FOR ANY TRADE.

CHEESEMAN & SON FURNITURE REMOVERS Whitton HOUNSLOW.
CHEESEMAN & SON REMOVERS & HAULAGE CONTRACTORS

Actual Size 7 ft. 6 in × 3 ft.

ANY DESIGN, HOWEVER ELABORATE, CAN BE INCLUDED.

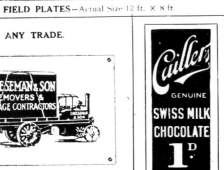

Cailler's
GENUINE
SWISS MILK
CHOCOLATE
1 D.
PACKET

5½ in. × 13½ in.

E. BECKETT & Co.
ESTD 1876

Shaped Plate.

WALTER MOORE & Co

Bent Plate.

OUR COMPLETE CATALOGUE POST FREE ON RECEIPT OF TRADE CARD.

Reduced Illustrations of a few cheap and effective forms of Advertising as supplied to the Leading Advertisers.

ADVERTISING FINGER PLATES
ENAMELLED IRON.
One Quarter size – Actual Size.
2⅞ × 8½ in.)

ADVERTISING MATCH STRIKERS.
ENAMELLED IRON.
(One Quarter size Actual Size,
2⅙ × 8½ in.)

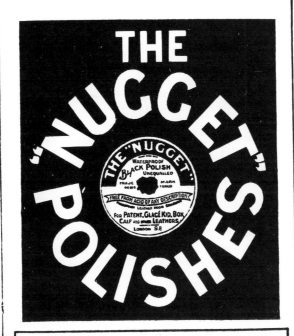

The above is a Reduced Illustration of a Specimen Set of Enamelled Copper Letters with Enamelled Medallion Fixed on Agents and Shopkeepers Windows throughout the United Kingdom and many places Abroad.   Considerably over ONE MILLION of these Letters have been supplied by us to Messrs. THE NUGGET POLISH Co.

See also Pages 6 and 52.

ENAMELLED IRON ADVERTISING PLATES.

SINGLE SIDED
MADE IN ANY SIZE OR DESIGN.

One-third size—Actual Size 9 × 3 in.

DOUBLE-SIDED WITH FLANGE
MADE IN ANY SIZE UP TO 24 × 18-in.

OPAL TABLETS
————
ABSOLUTELY
PERMANENT
AS SUPPLIED TO THE
LEADING ADVERTISERS.

Contracts undertaken for supplying and fixing these and similar plates throughout the United Kingdom at an Inclusive charge.

EXAMPLES OF PICTORIAL AND OTHER ENAMELLED IRON TABLETS FOR ADVERTISING.

IN ANY NUMBER OF COLOURS.

BOVRIL

WATSON'S MATCHLESS CLEANSER SOAP

MADE TO ANY SIZE.

BROOKE, BOND'S TEA

Perfect and Up-to-Date Plant for Rapid and Economical Production

DESIGNS and PRICES on APPLICATION.

Suchard's COCOA

DEWAR'S PERTH WHISKY

TOWER TEA

The examples of Pictorial Enamelled Tablets on this page are intended to shew the usual poster design, adapted to the permanent form of Enamelled Advertisement. The advantages of displaying to the public, for lengthy periods, a neat, cleanly and artistic poster design on a ceramic base, has already been clearly proved from an economical standpoint.

This cover and the following pages are from the pattern books of the Chromographic Enamel Co.
Approximate dates are given, and it can be seen that similar designs were produced over several decades.

No. 1.—12 × 8 ins.

No. 2.—17 × 12 ins.

No. 3.—60 × 40 ins.

No. 4.—11 × 9 ins.

No. 5.—17 × 12 ins.

No. 6.—36 × 10 ins.

No. 7.—35 × 7½ ins.

No. 8.—42 × 21 ins.

No. 9.—30 ins. square.

No. 10.—18 × 12 ins.
LETTERED BOTH SIDES.

No. 11.—18 × 12 ins.

ELECTRIC LIGHTING
BY
W. R. Brown.
LONDON.

No. 120.—24×18 ins.

No. 121 N.—32×34 ins.

HUDSON'S DRY SOAP

Used in all the "Happy Homes of England"

HUDSON'S

No. 122.—32×42 ins.

Milkmaid
BRAND
Milk
LARGEST SALE IN THE WORLD

As a Guarantee of Quality see the
Milkmaid on every Tin

TRADE MARK

No. 125.—43×96 in.

JONES AND HIGGINS, LTD

DRAPERS AND PECKHAM

HOUSE FURNISHERS LONDON. S.E

No. 126.—96×42 ins.

ROYAL
ROYAL INSURANCE COMPANY
INSURANCE
FIRE AGENCY
CO.

No. 127.—36×24 ins.

"Vinolia" Soap
FOR SENSITIVE SKINS
FOR TOILET, NURSERY & BATH

No. 128.—39×20 ins.

USE
SPECIAL MANURES for all CROPS
PLYMOUTH

No. 129.
12×24 ins.

PICNIC Brand CONDENSED MILK

No. 130.—18×24 ins.

USE
"CORN & GRASS" MANURES
PLYMOUTH

No. 131.
12×24 ins.

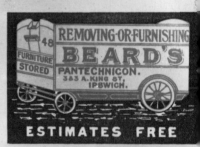

REMOVING·OR·FURNISHING
BEARD'S
PANTECHNICON.
3&5 A. KING ST.,
IPSWICH.
48 FURNITURE STORED
ESTIMATES FREE

No. 132.—36×24 ins.

FOR THE PEOPLE.
IN PACKETS
MFL
HUDSON'S SOAP
IN FINE POWDER
ESTABLISHED OVER 50 YEARS.

No. 103.—38×28 ins.

LIPTON'S
THE FINEST TEA THE WORLD PRODUCES.

No. 104 N.—72×36 ins.

Lifebuoy Soap
DISINFECTS WHILE CLEANSING

No. 105 N.—72×48 ins.

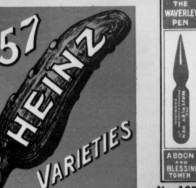

57 HEINZ VARIETIES

No. 108 N.—36×42 ins.

THE WAVERLEY PEN
THE WAVERLEY PEN
A BOON AND BLESSING TO MEN

No. 107 N.
5×24 ins.

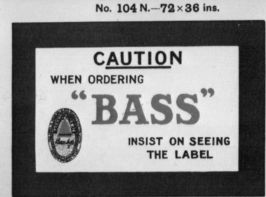

CAUTION
WHEN ORDERING
"BASS"
INSIST ON SEEING THE LABEL

No. 109 N.—60×40 ins.

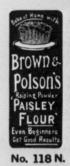

Bake at Home with
Brown & Polson's
Raising Powder
PAISLEY FLOUR
Even Beginners Get Good Results.

No. 118 N.
4×10 ins.

Fry's
PURE CONCENTRATED
COCOA AND MILK CHOCOLATE
300 GRANDS PRIX. GOLD MEDALS &c.

No. 110 N.—30×45 ins.

ZEBRA Grate Polish
Easy Work

No. 111.—14×8 ins.

HUDSON'S FOR THE PEOPLE

No. 113.—15½×7½ ins.

ABSTRACT
COAL MINES REGULATION ACTS, 1887 to 1908.

No. 114.—20×33 ins.
(Also "Quarries Act.")

WILLS'S
GOLD FLAKE CIGARETTES
10 FOR 3 D½
In Packets Only
W.D. & H.O. WILLS, BRISTOL & LONDON
CIGARETTES SOLD HERE.

No. 115 N.—18×36 ins.

EXPLOSIVES' ACT, 1875.
CLAUSE 77.

"Any Person who enters without permission, or otherwise trespasses upon any Factory, Magazine, or Store, or the Land immediately adjoining thereto, which is occupied by the occupier of such Factory, Magazine or Store, or on any Wharf, for which Bye-laws are made by the occupier thereof under this Act, shall, for every offence, if not otherwise punishable, be liable to a penalty not exceeding Five Pounds, and may be forthwith removed from such Factory, Magazine, Store, Land,.or Wharf, by any Constable, or by the occupier of such Factory, Magazine, Store, or Wharf,or any agent, or servant of, or other person authorised by such occupier."

"Any Person other than the occupier of or Person in or about any Factory, Magazine, or Store, who is found committing any act which tends to cause Explosion or Fire in or about such Factory, Magazine, or Store, shall be liable to a penalty not exceeding Fifty Pounds."

No. 116 N.—14×24 ins.

VAN HOUTEN'S COCOA

No. 117 N.—84×48 ins.

Wood Milne
RUBBER HEELS

No. 119 N.—24×10 ins.

BEST SOAPS FOR TOILET HOUSEHOLD AND STABLE

NORTH WEST SOAP COMPY. LIMITED CALCUTTA AND MEERUT

No. 82.—42×36 ins.

ZEBRA GRATE POLISH

No. 84 N.—20×30 ins.

APPOINTED BY SPECIAL ROYAL WARRANT

SOAP MAKERS TO HER MAJESTY THE QUEEN

SUNLIGHT SOAP

No. 83.—36×24 ins.

BRASSO METAL POLISH.

No. 85 N.—36×8 ins.

graphic Address "CTORY

Catalogues Free on application

DE VILLE & CO. VEHICLE MANUFACTURERS PAARL

No. 88.—48×36 ins.

Stephen's Inks

150 140 130 120 110 100 90 80 70 60 50 40 30 20 10

FEVER HEAT
BLOOD HEAT
SUMMER HEAT
TEMPE-RATE
FREEZ-ING

For all Temperatures

Stephen's Inks

No. 89. (Three sizes.)

BOVRIL

No. 86 N.—48×15 ins.

940

No. 93.—9×6½ ins.

4352 CONDUCTOR

No. 94.—4¼×3½ ins.

STAGE 19,565 DRIVER

No. 95.—4¼×3½ ins.

75

No. 96.—3×2 ins.

3

No. 97. 2½×1½ ins.

20

No. 98.—6×4 ins.

1521

No. 99.—3¾×1⅞ ins.

CWTS 21 QRS 3

No. 90.—6×3 ins. CART TARE FRAME.

KEEP TO THE RIGHT

No. 91.—5×6½ ins. Lettered both sides.

467

No. 92. 3½×2½ ins.

Spike 9 ins. long.

10

No. 100.—3¾×2½ ins.

30

No. 101 —4×2¾ ins.

40

No. 102.—5×3 ins.

ROBIN STARCH
EQUAL TO RECKITTS BLUE

No. 1 N.—10×12 ins.

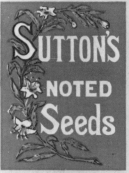

SUTTON'S NOTED Seeds

No. 2.—12×17 ins.

THE CORNISH RIVIERA

GREAT WESTERN RAILWAY.

MAXIMUM OF SUNSHINE.

EQUABLE TEMPERATURE

WINTER —AND— SUMMER.

Illustrated Travel Book. Post Free 3d apply. Superintendent of the Line Paddington Station, London. JAMES C INGLIS General Manager

ENGLAND'S NATIONAL HEALTH & PLEASURE RESORT.

No. 3 N.—14×12 ins. and 42×36 ins.

GOODALL'S CUSTARD POWDER
MAKES DELICIOUS CUSTARD WITHOUT EGGS
IN BOXES 6D & 1/ EACH
GOODALL, BACKHOUSE & CO LEEDS

No. 4.—11×9 ins.

WEBBS' SEEDS
WORDSLEY. STOURBRIDGE

No. 5 N.—24×36 ins.

GUANO OHLENDORFF'S MANURES

No. 8.—42×21 ins.

USE SUNLIGHT SOAP

No. 9.—30 ins. square.

AGENT FOR P&P Campbell cleaners PERTH

No. 10 N.—20×24 ins.
Lettered both sides.

COCOA & CHOCOLATE
ROWNTREE'S CHOCOLATES AND PASTILLES
MAKERS TO H M THE KING

No. 11 N.—20×30 ins.

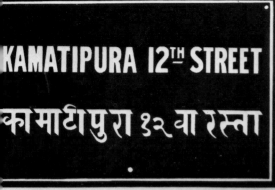

KAMATIPURA 12TH STREET

कामाटीपुरा १२ वा रस्ता

F. 17.   24×15 ins.

AGENTUR
for
Ulykkesforsikrings Selskabet
NOVA.
i HAAG.(HOLLAND)

F. 19.   10×8 ins.

شارع التربة

CHAREH
EL TOURBAH

F. 18.   24×16 ins.

BELGISCH
TOL KANTOOR

DOUANE BELGE

F. 21.   17×21½ ins.

पैखाना।
পাইখানা।

F. 20.   20×14½ ins.

JALAN
UNGKOO
ANDOT

F. 22.   19½×6¼ ins.

Colman's Blue.

F. 23.   36×36 ins.

WINDOW DELIVERY
এইখানে ডাক বিলি হয়

F. 24.   22×7½ ins.

BRODIES ROAD
பி ரூடஸ் சாலே

F. 25.   30×9 ins.

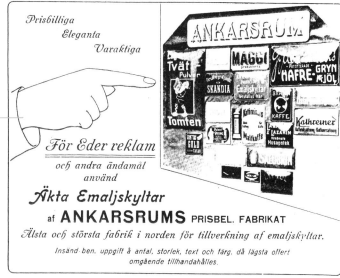

Prisbilliga
Eleganta
Varaktiga

För Eder reklam
och andra ändamål
använd

Äkta Emaljskyltar
af **ANKARSRUMS** PRISBEL. FABRIKAT

Älsta och största fabrik i norden för tillverkning af emaljskyltar.

Insänd ben. uppgift å antal, storlek, text och färg. då lägsta offert omgående tillhandahålles.

A page from Swedish manufacturers Ankarsrums catalogue, turn of the century.

MANUFACTURERS OF ENAMEL ADVERTISING SIGNS

The following is a list of known major manufacturers, past and present, plus a selection of their clients when possible and dates of signs where known.

Company	Location	Product
Artemail	Brussels, Belgium	Spa, Martini
Bruton	London	Lyons, Tea, Fremlins Lager
*Burnham	London	Tizer, Frys
Chromographic	Wolverhampton	Hudsons Soap, Frys 5 Boys, Milkmaid (c.1890), Stranges Oil, Coopers Remedy (Spanish)
*Enamelled Iron	Oldbury	
Ewwisons	Birmingham	
Falkirk Iron	Falkirk	Mobil, Chairman Tobacco
Franco	London	Pratts Motor Spirit (1923)
*Garnier	London	Typhoo Tea, Cadburys, Van Houten's Nosegay
Griffiths & Browett		Brooke Bond Tea
Griffiths & Millington	London & Birmingham	Danes Anchor Brewery, Ambrose Kid Gloves
Imperial	Birmingham	
Jordon & Sons	Bilston	Stephens Ink Thermometer (1913), Cooperative Society
*Madras Enamel	Madras, India	
Peco	Birmingham	Volkswagen (1959)
Protector	Eccles	BP Motor Spirit (Union Jack), Filtrate Oils
Patent Enamel	London & Birmingham	Quaker Oats (c.1890), Colmans Mustard & Starch (1929), Fry's Cocoa (c.1900), Whites Ginger Beer, Phipps Ale, Elliman's Embrocation (c.1890)
Stainton & Hulme	Birmingham	Players Navy Cut
Stocal Enamels	Burton & Birmingham	Ediswan Lamps, Shell, Guinness
Wildman & Maguyer	London	Sturmy Archer, Mobiloil, Triumph Cycles, Lyons Tea, Nestlés Milk
Willings	London	
Woodfield	London	
Wood & Penfold	London	Thorleys Pig Food

British and American editions of Street Jewellery and its Continental versions, a poster for the Street Jewellery exhibition, wallpaper by Crown and wrapping paper by Elgin Court Designs.

The Authors.

The authors and Street Jewellery

Christopher Baglee and Andrew Morley were pioneers of enamel sign collecting in the 1960s, and through their exhibition and their books 'Street Jewellery' and 'More Street Jewellery', they have established the collecting of enamel advertising signs as an accepted form of specialist collecting, joining ranks with those other recently established collectables bottles, motorabilia, decorative tins and cigarette packs. The term 'street jewellery' which they coined, has now been enshrined in the English language by inclusion in the O.E.D.

Christopher and Andrew joined forces in 1975, and their comprehensive collection soon became so well known throughout the North of England that by 1977 they were asked to mount an exhibition of 150 of their best enamel advertising signs, with loans from other private collections. This was first displayed in Newcastle upon Tyne in April 1978, and due to its instant success the exhibition made a national tour of 18 cities around Great Britain until June 1980. The catalogue produced for this exhibition formed the basis for the first book on the subject of enamel signs, 'Street Jewellery'. The books have firmly established the authors as leading authorities on the collecting and history of enamel signs. In this capacity they write features for national periodicals, and continue to collect material and information, and to research the subject for publication. Their collection, now referred to as Street Jewellery, is on permanent public display in the Linden Hall Pub, in the grounds of the Linden Hall Hotel, Longhorsley, Northumberland.

In 1983 Christopher and Andrew founded the Street Jewellery Society for the benefit of collectors of enamel signs, both in Great Britain and abroad.

Since the publication of the books, the domestic consumer market and the gift trade have produced many interesting products featuring enamel signs as their theme or basic design. Actual reproduction of original signs has been carried out by Relic Designs, Garnier Gifts and Goldie Repros. Other items incorporating enamel sign designs include the colourful sheets of wrapping paper and wall posters by Elgin Court Designs, a range of ready pasted vinyl wallpapers by Crown, and a series of railway modellers' miniature card versions of enamels by Tiny Signs. It seems that there is a wide application for the re-use of these old enamel designs in the modern nostalgia market, and we avidly await further developments.

4D 4OZ TINS. 8OZ TINS 8D

NATURAL HEALTH SALT

MANUFACTURED BY

WILKINSON & SIMPSON LTD

AT THEIR LABORATORY
24, NEWGATE ST
NEWCASTLE on TYNE

STIMULATES the LIVER, CURES BILIOUS HEADACHE, CLEARS the BRAIN.

CHURCHMAN'S NOTED COUNTER SHAG

In Packets only. The best lasts longest.

LOCH CORRIE

"REAL SCOTCH"

A HAPPY BLEND OF OLD MALT WHISKY

MARSHALL & ELVY LTD London & Glasgow

"The Friendly Light"

THOMPSON'S WALMER BREWERY

ASK YOUR CHEMIST FOR

"YOUR FIRST AID"

CALVEX

BRAND

CARBOLIC

OINTMENT

F.C. CALVERT & CO LTD MANCHESTER

"YOUR FIRST AID"

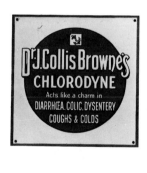

1D A GLASS 1D

VANTAS

SPARKLING DRINKS

Chairman Cigarettes are always better.

R.J. Lea Ltd. Manchester

WORTHINGTON'S

BREWERS BY APPOINTMENT

TO HIS MAJESTY THE KING

INDIA PALE ALE

TRADE MARK

BURTON ON TRENT

THIS LABEL IS ISSUED ONLY BY WORTHINGTON & CO LTD

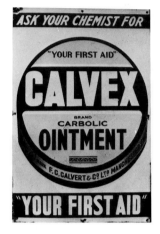

MURPHY

MAKING WIRELESS SIMPLE

DR J. Collis Browne's

CHLORODYNE

Acts like a charm in

DIARRHŒA, COLIC, DYSENTERY COUGHS & COLDS

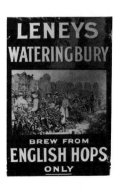

LENEYS WATERINGBURY

BREW FROM ENGLISH HOPS ONLY

GOLD COX'S MEDALS

ANTI-BURTON

THE ORIGINAL TEMPERANCE ALE

K...s CROSS. LONDON. N.

By the authorities on Modern Science

Odol

has been proved the best for Mouth and Teeth

PLAYER'S NAVY MIXTURE

PIPE PERFECT

Bibliography

Enamel Advertising Signs:
'Blechplakate', Axel Riepenhausen, F. Coppenrath,
1979 (Germany).
'Email-Borden', Jaques Stakenborg & Jaap van Zadelhoff,
Uitgeverij de Viergang, 1979 (Holland).
'Email-Plakate', Ulrich Feuerhorst & Holger Steinle,
Harenberg, 1981 (Germany).
'Enamelled Street Signs', Christopher Baglee &
Andrew Morley, Everest House, 1978 (U.S.A.).
'La Plaque Emaillee Publicitaire', Michel Wlassikoff,
Editions Alternatives, 1985 (France).
'More Street Jewellery', Christopher Baglee &
Andrew Morley, New Cavendish Books, 1982 (England).
'Street Jewellery', Christopher Baglee & Andrew Morley,
New Cavendish Books, 1978 (England).
'Svenska Skyltar', Birgitta Conradson & Olle Nessle,
LT's, 1980 (Sweden).

Enamels in Context:
'A Fortune in Your Attic', Tony Curtis (Ed),
Lyle Publications, 1985 (Scotland).
'Automobilia', Michael Worthington-Williams,
Batsford/RAC, 1979 (England).
'Cash in on Collecting', Tony Curtis (Ed),
Lyle Publications, 1986 (Scotland).
'Collector's Year Book 1977', Gordon Litherland & Ian
Waterfield (Eds), M.A.B. Publishing, 1977 (England).
'Price Guide to Collectibles', Tony Curtis (Ed),
Lyle Publications, 1984 (Scotland).

General Advertising:
'The Advertising Book', The History of Advertising in
Ireland', Hugh Oram, MO Books, 1986 (Ireland).
'Advertising in Britain', T. R. Nevett,
Heinemann, 1982 (England).
'The Art of Advertising', Bryan Holme,
Peerage Books, 1985 (England).
'The Art of the Label', Robert Opie, Simon and Schuster,
1987 (England).
'British Biscuit Tins 1868–1939', M. J. Franklin,
New Cavendish Books, 1979 (England).
'Bubbles', Mike Dempsey (Ed), Fontana, 1978 (England).
'Cigarette Pack Art', Chris Mullen,
Hamlyn, 1979 (England).
'Cocoa & Corsets', Michael Jubb,
HMSO, 1984 (England).
'Collecting for Tomorrow', Brian Jewell,
Blandford Press, 1979 (England).
'Decorative Printed Tins', David Griffith,
Studio Vista, 1979 (England).
'Ephemera of Travel and Transport', Janice Anderson &
Edmund Swinglehurst, New Cavendish Books, 1981
(England).
'Guinness Advertising', Brian Selby,
Guinness Books, 1985 (England).
'The History of Bovril Advertising', Peter Hadley (Ed),
Bovril Ltd., 1971 (England).
'Package & Print', Alec Davis,
Faber & Faber, 1967 (England).

McNiven & Cameron premises from 'Colin Baxter's Edinburgh'.

'Pipe Dreams', Mike Dempsey (Ed),
Pavilion, 1982 (England).
'Rule Britannia', Robert Opie, Viking, 1985 (England).
'Slogans', Nigel Rees,
George Allen & Unwin, 1982 (England).
'The Story of Sunlight', Edmund Williams,
Unilever, 1984 (England).
'Taking Stock', Penny Vincenzi,
Collins Willow, 1985 (England).
'The Tin Can Book', Hyla M. Clark,
The New American Library, 1977 (USA).
'Victorian Advertisements', Leonard de Vries & James
Laver, John Murray, 1968 (England).
'The Wonderful World of Coca-Cola', Martin Shartar &
Norman Shavin, Perry Communications, 1981 (USA).

Bass Museum, Burton on Trent, Notts.
Beamish North of England Open Air Museum, Stanley,
Co. Durham.
Black Country Museum, Dudley, West Midlands.
Bluebell Railway, Uckfield, Sussex.
Brewhouse Yard Museum, Nottingham, Notts.
Castle Museum, York, Yorkshire.
Colman's Museum, Norwich, Norfolk.
Cotswolds Motor Museum, Bourton-on-the-Water,
Gloucestershire.
Ironbridge Gorge Museum, Telford, Shropshire.
Keighley & Worth Valley Railway, Keighley, Yorkshire.
Kelham Island Industrial Museum, Sheffield, Yorkshire.
Landmark Centre, Stirling, Stirlingshire.
Lavender Line Railway, Sussex.
Linden Hall Hotel, Longhorsley, Northumberland.
London Toy & Model Museum, Paddington.
Museum of Transport, Pollokshields, Glasgow.
Myreton Motor Museum, Aberlady, East Lothian.
National Motor Museum, Beaulieu, Hampshire.
North Yorkshire Moors Railway, Vale of Pickering.
Pack Age Museum, Albert Warehouse, Gloucester
Docks, Gloucestershire.
Preston Hall Museum, Stockton on Tees, Cleveland.
Scolton Manor, near Haverfordwest, Pembrokeshire,
Wales.
Severn Valley Railway, Bristol, Avon.
Strathspey Railway, Aviemore.
Ulster Folk & Transport Museum, Cultraw, Belfast.

Index

Page numbers for colour signs have a C prefix.

Crow Bar Tobacco, C6
C.W.S. Congress Soap, C4

Dagenite Accumulators, C12
Daily Mirror, The, 20, 25, C16
Daily Sketch, C6
Daily Telegraph, C16
Danish Dairy Co., 98
Dartnell's Ginger Beer, 68, C21
Davis Dyers & Cleaners, 68
Day & Martin's Polishes, C15
Dean, A. R., Bedsteads, C5
Deslespaul-Havez Chocolat, C8
Desmarais Motor Oil, 80
Dr. J. Collis Browne's Chlorodyne, 99
Duckams Adcoids, 70
Duckams Oils, C18

Ediswan Lamp Bulbs, 26, C5, C14
Edwards Desiccated Soup, C3
Eley Kynoch Cartridges, C23
Elliman's Embrocation, C17
Engrais d'Auby, 80, C8
Epp's Cocoa, 24, 26
Essolube, C6
Ex-Lax, C10
Ex-Ox Food Extract, 68

Feathery Flake Flour, 62
Field, The, 64
Finlay's Soap, C1
Firestone Tyres, 70
Ford, 23, 81
Forest Hill Beers, 69
Fram Razors, 75
Fraser Ltd., R. D. & J. B., C9
Fremlins Ale, 58, 71
Fry's Chocolate, 9, 13, 22, 31, 63, 78, C1, C15, C16
Fry's Cocoa, 12, 24, 26, 27, 30, 59, C18
Fry's Five Boys Chocolate, 17, 31, 32, 74, C10, C11

Gallaher's Cigarettes, C1
Glaxo, 81
Golden Penny, The, 68
Golliberry, see Robertson's
Good Bros. Builders Merchants, C7
Goodlass, Wall & Co Paints, 75
Goodyear, C15, C18, C19
Goss Porcelain, 58
Gossages' Dry Soap, 25, 68, C11
G.P. Government Tea, 27
Graf, 63
Green & Leddicott's, 68
Greys Cigarette, C7
Guinness, 68, C17, C18, C20

Haecht Beer, 79
Halifax Building Society, C4
Hall's Distemper, C21
Haputine for Headache, 62
Hardtmuth's 'Koh-I-Noor' pencils, 75
Hay, P & R, Cleaners, 31, 32, 59, 62, 63, C14
Heinz Tomato Chutney, 6
Heinz 57 Varieties, C2
Henko, 81
Hercules Cycles, 75
Herold Krauterlikor, 81
His Master's Voice, C17
Hoffmann's Starch, 98
Holdfast Boots, C7
Holzapfels Compositions, 65, 66, C20
Hop Leaf Ale, 57
Horniman's Tea, 27

Hovis Bread Flour Co., 13
Hudson Cycles, 24, 75, C1
Hudsons Removals & Storage, C2
Hudson's Soap, 13, 25, 26, 59, 68, 74, C1, C2, C4, C5, C6, C7, C9–11, C14, C17
Huntley & Palmers, C23
Husqvarna Motorcyhlar, C8

I & C, 27
Imperial Enamel Co. Ltd., C1
'In Brandstoften', C19
Ingersoll Watches, 9, C22
Invalid Chairs, 75
Iron Jelloids, 20
Ironclad Mantles, 63

James Dome Black Lead, 26
Jes-Dene Fruit Crushes, 62
Jeyes' Fluid Disinfectant, C5
Jeyes' Sheep Dip, 71
John Bull, C1
Johnnie Walker Whisky, C4
Jones' Sewing Machines, 31, 32, C20
Jude & Co's Pale Ale, 69

Karpol Car Polish, 59, C9
Kentish Hop Garden, 99
Kenya Beer, C13
Kodak Film, 58
Komo Metal Paste, 26, C18
Kop's Crisps, C6
Kronenbrau, C8
Kub Bouillon, C8

Lactifer for Calves, 98
Lambert & Butler's Rhodian Curly Cut, C4
Lazarol & Lazarin, 65
Leney's Wateringbury, 99
Leno, J. & Sons, Removals, C21
Lifebuoy Soap, 71
Lipton's Tea, 27
Lissen Mica Plugs, C20
Little's Sheep Dip, C3
Littlewoods Depot, C10
Lloyd's News, 78
Loch Corrie Malt Whisky, 99
Lucas Batteries, 25, 59, C15
Lucas Spades, 63, C20
Lyon's Cakes, 59
Lyon's Cocoa, 26, C3
Lyons' Ink, C16
Lyon's Pies, C11
Lyon's Tea, 25, 27, 59, 68, 71, C15, C23

Macdonalds Cut Golden Bar, C3
MacNiven & Cameron Pens, 74, C10
McDougal's Flour, C1
Maestrani Chocolate, 80
Maggi, 80, 81, C8
'Mangling Done Here', 26
Maple & Co, 13
Marmet Pram, The, C6
Martini, C19
Matchless Metal Polish, 75, 98, C9, C20
Mazawattee Tea, 13, 20, 27, 57, 58, 71, C21
Melox Dog Foods, C17
Melrose's Tea, 27
Menier Chocolate, 80, C8
Milkmaid 'Cafe au Lait', 27, C6
Milkmaid Milk, C18
Mitchells and Butlers' Ales, C13
Mobiloil, 23, 58, C14, C19
Monschshof Brau, 80

Monsters Pop, 70, C2, C21
Mont Blanc Milk, 80
Morgans Ale & Stout, 69
Morris Cars, 59, 68, 74
Morris Service, C13, C20
Morris's Blue Book Cigarettes, C2
Morse's Distemper, 31, 32
Murphy, 99
Murrays' Mottled Flake, C5

National Benzole Mixture, C11
National Building Society, C7
Nectar Tea, 13, 25, 27, 58, 63, C20
Nestle's Milk, 59, C19
New Hudson Bicycles, C1
News of the World, The, 79
New Zealand Insurance Co., 80
Nicolas, 80
Nile Spinning & Doubling Co. Ltd., 12
Nosegay Tobacco and Cigarettes, 62, 71, 78, C23
Nuggett Boot Polish, 21, 78, C4
Nut Brown, C2

Oceanic Accident & Guarantee, The, C5
Oceanic Footwear, 58
Odol, 99
Ogden's Battle Axe Bar, C17, C22
Ogden's Cigarettes, 62, 73, 79
Ogden's Cobnut Tobacco, 68
Ogden's Coolie Cut Plug, C21, C22
Ogden's Guinea Gold Cigarettes, C4
Ogden's Redbreast Flake, C18
Ogden's St. Bruno, C9, C16
Ogden's St. Julien, C3, C9, C16
Ogden's Walnut Plug, C17, C20, C23
Old Navy Rum, C6
Omara's Bacon & hams, C7
Ovaltine, C13
Ovum, 20, C18
Oxo, 24, 60, C8, C9, C10, C17

Page & Overtons Oatmeal Stout, C4
Palethorpes, 31, 59, 62, 63, 74, C4, C11, C12
Palmer Cord Tyres, 23
Parapluie Revel, C8
Parkinsons Pills, 57
Pascall's Confectionery, 63
Passing Show, The, C3
Patent Enamel Co, C3

Patent Steam Carpet Beating Co Ltd, C13
Pather Iron & Steel Company, 16
Pear's Soap, 13, 24, C1
Pearson's Weekly, 64
Pelaw Liquid Metal Polish, C23
People Sunday Paper, The, 7
Pepsi Cola, C19
Persil, 80, 81, C8
Perlesreuter, C8
Petre de Vos brewery, 79
Petter's Oil, 74, C23
Pfaff Sewing Machines, 80
Philips, 58
Phillips Cocoa, 27
Phillips Tea, C4
Phipps Diamond Ale, C18
Pickerings, C4
Pickfords & Co, 75, C2
Pioneer Cement, C16
Player's Airman, 62, C20
Player's Country Life Tobacco, 71
Player's Drumhead Cigarettes, C18
Player's Navy Cut, 31, 68, C3, C11, C14
Player's Navy Mixture, 99, C13
Player's Please, C12, C22
Pratt's, C23
Pratt's Lamp Oil, 26
Pratt's Motor Oil, 23
Pratt's Motor Spirit, 23
Price's Motor Oil, C6
Prices Night Lights, 75
Public Benefit Boot Company, 73
Punch, 64, C3
Puritan Leather Soles, 32
Puritan Soap, C7

Quaker Oats, 6, C6, C7, C15
Queen, The, 64

Rajah Cigars, C2, C16
Raleigh Bicycles, 58, 62, 74, 75, C13
Ransome's Farming Equipment, 20
Reckitt's, 21, 26, C13
Redbreast Flake, see Ogden's
Redfern's, 20
Redgate Table Waters, C20
Red-Ex, C4
Remington Typewriters, 75
Renault Cars, 59, C19
Restu Cleaner, 70
Rhein-Perle, C8
Ricard, 80
Rinso, 25, C10
Robbialac Paints, C2
Robertson's Golden Shred, C2
Robertson's Golliberry, C16